… **Playgrou…**

Let your creativity flow...

East & West Sussex
Edited by Gemma Hearn

First published in Great Britain in 2005 by:
Young Writers
Remus House
Coltsfoot Drive
Peterborough
PE2 9JX
Telephone: 01733 890066
Website: www.youngwriters.co.uk

All Rights Reserved

© Copyright Contributors 2005

SB ISBN 1 84602 174 X

Foreword

Young Writers was established in 1991 and has been passionately devoted to the promotion of reading and writing in children and young adults ever since. The quest continues today. Young Writers remains as committed to the fostering of burgeoning poetic and literary talent as ever.

This year's Young Writers competition has proven as vibrant and dynamic as ever and we are delighted to present a showcase of the best poetry from across the UK. Each poem has been carefully selected from a wealth of *Playground Poets* entries before ultimately being published in this, our thirteenth primary school poetry series.

Once again, we have been supremely impressed by the overall high quality of the entries we have received. The imagination, energy and creativity which has gone into each young writer's entry made choosing the best poems a challenging and often difficult but ultimately hugely rewarding task - the general high standard of the work submitted amply vindicating this opportunity to bring their poetry to a larger appreciative audience.

We sincerely hope you are pleased with our final selection and that you will enjoy *Playground Poets East & West Sussex* for many years to come.

Contents

Charters Ancaster College, Bexhill-on-Sea
Charlotte Thorkildsen (8)	1
Katie Reeve (8)	1
Patrick Pope (8)	2
Dale Watts (11)	2
Isobel Kellett (9)	3
Claire Younger (9)	3
Matthew Pope (11)	4
Katie Hatter (9)	5
Rosie Reeve (11)	6
Jack Kitchen (8)	6
Emma Bignell (11)	7
Danny Horton (8)	7
Stephen Kennedy-Redmile-Gordon (9)	8
Daisy Reece (10)	9

Fletching CE Primary School, Uckfield
Tristan King (7)	9
Brooke Sones (7)	10
Christopher St Denis (8)	10
Philip Fletcher (7)	10
Maysie Coe (7)	11
Anna Roe (8)	11
Lydia Bunyard (7)	11

Great Ballard School, Chichester
Anne Cole (11)	12
Sam Terry (10)	12
Hayley Mackay (10)	13
Oliver Coombe-Tennant (10)	13
Clara Butterworth (10)	14
Amelia Pickles (10)	14
Jessica Simmonds (10)	15
Elisa Castro (10)	15
Ysabelle Shopland (11)	16

Hellingly CP School, Hailsham
- Etienne Robinson-Sivyer (8) — 16
- Jack Moloney (11) — 17

Jessie Younghusband Primary School, Chichester
- Lucy Egleton (9) — 18
- Andrew Main (11) — 18
- Douglas Morrison (10) — 19
- Olivia Whatmore (10) — 19
- Samuel Peake (10) — 19
- Joy Horton (10) — 20
- Harriet Smith (10) — 20
- Rosie Little (11) — 20
- Toby White (9) — 21
- Rebecca Harrington (8) — 21
- Reuben Underhill (10) — 21
- Megan Gent (9) — 22
- Chloe Sellwood (10) — 22
- Andrew Creswick (9) — 23
- Katie Adams (8) — 23
- Abbey Lamb (8) — 24
- Georgina Warner (8) — 24
- Octavia Musumeci (9) — 25
- Hannah New (9) — 25

Little Common School, Bexhill-on-Sea
- Charlotte Russell (7) — 25
- Poppy Lelliott (9) — 26
- Elliott Leonard-Diss (9) — 26
- Fern Denney (9) — 27
- George Stinson (9) — 27
- William Templeton (7) — 28
- Azjad Elmubarak (8) — 28
- Ellis Evento (7) — 28
- Harry Saville (9) — 29
- Matthew Edwards (9) — 29
- Alexander Christodoulou (7) — 29
- Jack Taylor (10) — 30
- Ben Profit (10) — 30
- Toni Cearns (7) — 30

Lewis Kemp (9)	31
Sonya Sharma (7)	31
Sam Hodger (8)	31
Oscar Hammond (9)	32
Samuel Hills (10)	32
Liam Berriman (9)	33
Alice Geraghty (9)	33
Jonathan Corke (10)	34
Georgia Lea (9)	34
Matthew Middleton (9)	35
George Jeffery (9)	35
Jack Roadway (9)	36
Cameron Kirk (10)	36
Danielle Sellers (9)	36
Jack Vincent (10)	37
Darragh Groves (7)	37
Katie Moore (9)	37
Jazer Barclay (10)	38
Joshua Eaton (9)	38
Abbie Latasha Beale (9)	38
Cameron Smith (10)	39
Lydia Luck (9)	39
Andrew Slinn (9)	40
Jodie Boyle (9)	40
Callum Hall (9)	41
Toby Cowling (10)	41
Emma Jeffery (7)	42
Luke Whiting (10)	42
Lydia Harrison (7)	42
Milly Clifford (9)	43
Ben Stiles (9)	43

Milton Mount Primary School, Crawley

Dominic Henry (9)	43
Natalie Bale (11)	44
Rebecca Bala (10)	44
Masuma Shamsi (11)	45
Chelsey Wells (11)	45
Luke Knight (11)	46
Grant Bevis (10)	46
Kimali Brook (11)	47

Kiran Sajjan (11)	47
Alice Lloyd (7)	48
Jessica Davison (11)	48
Charlotte Cook (11)	49
Ella Marsh (7)	49
Kieran Fellows (10)	50
Georgia Davis (9)	50
Adele Morris (10)	50
Alexandra Karagoz (10)	51
Lee Marsh (10)	51
Sivalekha Viramuthu (9)	51
Eleanor Terry (8)	52
Amy Froshaug (10)	52
Georgia Amos (7)	53
Bradley Bell (7)	53
Alexander Lamm (10)	54
Connor Grant (8)	54
Kieran Armstrong (11)	55
Amy Johnson (7)	55
Sam Briggs (9)	56
Emily Hawkins (7)	56
Gurben Sra (7)	57
Beth Hicks (7)	57
Christopher Beaton (10)	58
Joel Lovelock (8)	58
Hayleigh Frith (10)	59
Suzie Galvin (8)	59
Georgia Welch (11)	60
Anand Lukhani (10)	60
Rae Degnan (11)	61
Chloe Homewood (8)	61
Robin Laney (10)	62
Hollie Lloyd (8)	62
Emma Harding (10)	63
Alana Cameron (8)	63
James Seymour (10)	64
Emily Wright (10)	64
Charlotte Milham (10)	65
Joe Gardiner (9)	65
Holly Talbut-Smith (8)	66
Pranay Patel (9)	66
Chloe Casey (11)	67

Georgie Baker (9)	67
Joshua Weaver (9)	68
Georgina Allen (11)	68
Charlotte Croft (11)	69
Emma Costello (9)	69
Emma Clark (10)	70
Bhavik Lakhani (9)	71
Stephen Gilchrist (10)	71
Matthew Keating (10)	72
Henry Yeomans (9)	72
Jodie Cashman (9)	72
Peter Warnock (10)	73
Blaise Salle (8)	73
Georgia Simmonds (9)	73
Haleigh Lembergs (8)	74
Nicole Laker (9)	74
Hannah Paton (10)	74
Emma Osborne (10)	75
Sophie Norris (9)	75
Karenjit Padda (10)	75
Rhys Freeman (10)	76
Kimberley Logan (11)	76
Katie Steed (11)	77

Ocklynge County Junior School, Eastbourne

Gabrielle Martin (8)	77
Kelly Snow (9)	78
Oska Eames (7)	78
Paul Blackwell (8)	79
Adelaide Morgan (7)	79
Meggie Dennis (8)	80
Antonia Fitzjohn (8)	81
Sarah Reading (7)	81
Pascale Smith (8)	81

Patcham House (Day Special) School, Brighton

Sophie Pengilly (10)	82
Harrison Austen-Evans (9)	82
Paris Carroll (7)	82
Jack Wright (11)	83
George Bolger (8)	83

Nathan Lovegrove (11)   84
Jamie Bourne (10)   84

Rose Green Junior School, Bognor Regis

Emily Waters (9)   84
Leah Minett (8)   85
Ellie Edwards (8)   85
Alice Bugeja (9)   86
Joe Woods (11)   86
Hayley Kent (10)   87
Victoria Halsey (10)   87
Chloe Archer (9)   88
Laura Gibbs (9)   88
Heather Curtis (8)   89
Hannah Stride (9)   89
Eleanor Jupp (10)   90
Bethany Hirons (10)   90
Hayley Jewson (11)   91
Kathryn Everington (9)   91
Ollie Greenlees (10)   92
Claudia Dickens (10)   93
Lottie Greenlees (7)   94
Brook Sharp (7)   95
Chris Cox (11)   96
India Ede (11)   96
Oliver Bateman (10)   97
Joseph Martin (8)   97
Ellis Georgeou (9)   98
Rosie Hemming (11)   99

St Mark's CE Primary School, Brighton

Charlotte Roberts (10)   99
Lacey Cole (10)   100
Charlotte Rolf (10)   100
Bethany Dahr (10)   101
Zoe Fortune (9)   101
Emma Holdway (9)   102
Courtney Moffett (9)   102
Lacie-May Snow (9)   103
Jessie-Ellen Rutson (10)   103
Katherine Jolly (9)   104

Lily Mateer (9) 104

St Nicolas CE Junior School, Portslade
Charlotte Ashurst (10) 105
Courtney Francis (9) 105
Rhiannon Breeze (9) 106
Zara Butt (10) 107
Ashley Lidbetter (9) 107
Kala Gallacher (9) 108
Elizabeth Dillistone (10) 109
Rosie Nicholson (9) 109
Abigale Oakley (10) 110
Hayley Hodges (9) 110
Holly Knight (11) 111
Elisa Belluscio (9) 111
Christina Cushing (9) 112
Toni-Louise Richardson (11) 112
Daisy Roberts (10) 113
Georgia McNealy (9) 113
Rebecca Canneaux (10) 114
Maisy Johnsen (9) 114
Maisie Chandler (10) 115
Holly Molloy (11) 115
Andrew Connacher (10) 116
Fern Ridge (9) 116
Laura Andrews (11) 117
Robert Phillips (10) 117
Jack Trimm (11) 118
Lizzie Walker (11) 119
Samuel Lawrence (11) 119
Kayleigh Elliott (10) 120
Chloe Parks (9) 121
Reece Ezobi (8) 121
Jake Lawman (9) 122
George Fenton (11) 122
Louis Elkhatib (9) 122
Abigail Moles (9) 123
Jack Moss (9) 123
Shane Boyce (8) 123
Nicole Garoghan (9) 124
Taylor Shorter (9) 124

Jack Copping (8)	124
Sammy Carden (10)	125

St Peter & St Paul CE Primary School, Bexhill-on-Sea

Lydia Bunn (11)	125
Lauren Inglis (10)	125
Max Pritchett-Page (11)	126
Rebecca Freshwater (10)	126
Savanna Smith (10)	127
David Ammoun (10)	127
Douglas Benge (11)	128
Oliver Howard (10)	128
Tom Payne (10)	128
Katherine Skeates (11)	129
Greg Anderson (11)	129
Kallista Owen (11)	129
Beverley Eatten (10)	130
Sophie McGinty (10)	130
Ashley Iddenden (10)	130
Samuel Ball (11)	131
Ian Coshall (10)	131
Katie Robson (11)	131
Jamie Edwards (11)	132
Thomas Routley (10)	132
Hannah Mabb (11)	133
Greg Thompson (10)	133

Shinewater Primary School, Eastbourne

Hannah Sibson (10)	134
Jodie Pescott (11)	134
Kadie Cox (10)	135
Harry Mannel (11)	135
Sophie Edwards (11)	136
Daniel McManus (10)	136
Rachel O'Reilly (11)	136
Laura Davies (10)	137
Alex Trussell (11)	137
Sofia Rebaudo (10)	137
Elise Vincent (11)	138
Riva Cassidy (10)	138
William Upton (10)	138

Charlotte Webb (10)	139
Amy Drummond (11)	139
Ellen Curd (11)	139
Popi Begum (11)	140
Thomas Avery (11)	140
Christopher Mockford (10)	141
Ashley Green (10)	141
Charlotte Wilkins (11)	142
Sadie Cain (10)	142

Sidlesham Primary School, Chichester

James McCrone (10)	142
Stephanie Golder (11)	143
Chloe Russell-Sharp (7)	143
Rachael Manley (8)	143
Victoria Lamb (10)	144
Lizzie Forbes (9)	144
Freddie Pickering (8)	145
Anna Rawlinson (9)	145
Sian Louise Tunnell (9)	146
Abbie-Rose Curbison (8)	147
Beau Sullivan (9)	147
Jasmine Coppin (10)	148
Tom Curbison (10)	148

The Oaks Primary School, Crawley

Shannon Williams (9)	148
Jason Harrold (10)	149
Adam Laker (10)	149
Rebecca Leach (9)	149
Amberley Hillyard (9)	150
Emily Harman (9)	150
Benjamin Hillyard (7)	151
Sarah Nash (9)	151
Heidi Walker (9)	152
Hannah Traylen (9)	152
Emily Mashiter (10)	153
Stacey Truss (9)	153
Alice Alderson (8)	154
Scott Lumley (10)	155
Oliver Smith (10)	155

Jodie Pemberton (9)   156

Tollgate Community Junior School, Eastbourne
Harry Hills (11)   156
Tyla Hobbs (11)   157
Katy Spokes (10)   157
Harley Buckwell (11)   158
Nadia Alam (9)   158
Ryan Dowding (11)   159
Tom Seath (10)   159
Chloe Humphreys (10)   160
Kiaya Pike (10)   160
Matthew Collett (10)   160
Harry Brabham (9)   161
Bayan Fenwick (11)   161

Vale First & Middle School, Worthing
Amy Mugridge (10)   161
Martin Brooks (8)   162
Daniel Parkman (8)   162
Verity Wakeling (7)   163
Laura Edgoose (10)   163
Lisa Whiting (9)   164
Emily Cartwright (9)   164
Natalia Gargaro (9)   165
Siobhan Stanbridge (9)   165
Georgia Linfield (10)   166
Danielle Rogers (11)   166
Elizabeth Saxony (11)   167
Sophie Baker (9)   167
Rebecca Lewis (11)   168
Adam Fitchett (9)   168
Stephanie Parkman (10)   168
Frances Roberts (10)   169
Becky Potiphar (10)   169
Chloe Slaughter (9)   169
Jessica Gilbert-McHugh (10)   170
Jasmine Street (10)   171
Rebecca Offer (11)   171
Rosalind Frayard-Smith (11)   171
Rachel Rooke (10)   172

Walberton & Binsted CE Primary School, Walberton
Georgina Morley (8)	172
Samuel Pierce (8)	173
James Baker (8)	173
Joshua Harris (9)	173
Elizabeth Baxter (9)	174
Alex Baker (8)	174
Megan Payne (9)	174
Edward Myers (9)	175
Poppy Crawford (8)	175

West Hove Junior School, Hove
Oliver Bower-Neville (9)	175
Isabella Millington (10)	176
Rushna Razak (10)	176
Eva Zaninetti (10)	177
Aurora Miller (10)	177
Rhiannon Adams (11)	178
Amy Pike (10)	178
Jade Widdick (11)	179
Eleanor Cottingham (10)	179
Sammy Valder (10)	180
Lucy Robinson (10)	180
Felix Boyce (9)	180
Summa Watson (9)	181
Lydia Pope (11)	181

Wisborough Green Primary School, Wisborough Green
Rebeka Howarth (7)	181
Kwame Noye (9)	182
Connor Worrell (9)	182
George Gibson (9)	183
Rachel Warwick (10)	183
Laura Appleton (8)	184
Henry Felton (7)	184
Ailish Fowler (8)	185
Lucy Donovan (11)	185
Joey Calder Smith (8)	186
Iona Spackman (10)	186
Lauren Napper (10)	187
Paddy Fowler (10)	187

Joely Santa Cruz (11)	188
Oliver Luddy (10)	188
Georgina Marfe (10)	189
Ollie Howarth (10)	189
Alice Groves (10)	190
Rosie Osmaston (10)	190
Katie Wells (9)	191
Zachary Voaden (11)	191
Isobel Dyer (7)	192
Jonathan Maunders (10)	192
Edwina Lywood (7)	193
Laura Mackinnon (11)	193
Daniel MacDonald (10)	194
Lucy Boxall (10)	194
Laura Parker (8)	194
Lucy McLoughlin (7)	195
Paul Slade (11)	195
Tammy Harris (9)	195
Lucy Ansell (7)	196
Lise Easton (8)	196
Mark Slade (8)	196
Jade Osmaston (8)	197
Oscar Voaden (8)	197
Finn Spackman (8)	197
Maxim Dillon (7)	198
George Steere (8)	198
Ben Dadswell (11)	199
Violet Nicholls (7)	199
Ami Gilfoyle (7)	200
Richard Mason (8)	200
Charlotte Gay (7)	201
Jason Grove (7)	201
Emily Usher (8)	202
Tom Appleton (11)	202

The Poems

The Fairies

Down at the bottom of the garden
Underneath the cherry tree
There are some little folk
But you may not believe me.

There are rainbow fairies, weather fairies
Flower fairies too
All are friends with the honeybees
That make honey for me and you.

The king and queen sit high above
You'll find them drinking tea,
Watching the dancing fairies
As funny as can be.

So when the snow falls and you're in bed
Snuggly and warm
Think of the little folk
Hiding in the storm.

Then the spring fairy comes and
Makes the snow go away
Just by waving her magic wand
And that saves the day.

Charlotte Thorkildsen (8)
Charters Ancaster College, Bexhill-on-Sea

The Volcano

The volcano slithers
like a curling, looping snake
exploding from a tunnel.
It spits hot lava
dripping down like a glowing fire
of gold and silver butterflies.
White as the moon
it reflects the spangle and glitter of fireworks
and then sets to a rock
the colour of ash.

Katie Recve (8)
Charters Ancaster College, Bexhill-on-Sea

Under The Sea

The octopus is tender
Swimming like a twisty, wriggling jellyfish
Its slime flashes in the flaring sun.

The crab scuttles on the ocean floor,
Scampering carefully
Unseen as it crawls
Into its hole.

The amoeba, a small sponge
A squishy blue ball of jelly.
Its crafty movement
Takes it slyly away.

The clamshell
Stubborn and flinty
Waits for a squirmy shrimp
And *snap!*

Patrick Pope (8)
Charters Ancaster College, Bexhill-on-Sea

Contrasts

Loneliness is emptiness
The colour blue
An empty room
Friendless
Neglected by others
A mind full of nothing.

Friendliness is yellow
It is kindness
An encouraging crowd
Cheering others
Playing and sharing
A mind full of happiness.

Dale Watts (11)
Charters Ancaster College, Bexhill-on-Sea

Weather

Rain is sadness,
The colour grey.
When nothing goes straight
Will it forever rain?

Sun is a teacher's pet
Bright and boasting
Dazzling and sparkling
But casting shadows across the ground.

Thunder and lightning
Are twins
Following each other around.
They are the school bullies
Creeping up and pouncing!

But snow is a bright white carpet,
Fairies dancing delicately
Leading to unimagined
Worlds.

Isobel Kellett (9)
Charters Ancaster College, Bexhill-on-Sea

The Unicorn

If I were an artist
I would paint a unicorn.
For his head
I'd use silky, purple fur.

For his body
I'd have a flowery rainbow
And his hooves
Would be polished stones.

Then for his tail
I'd use glittery, sparkling thread
And for his horn
I'd need a sharp, silver sword.

Claire Younger (9)
Charters Ancaster College, Bexhill-on-Sea

Fear

I'm afraid of the dark
Are you?
A creaking door,
An awful storm
A dreadful wind.
Fear is my own worst enemy
Like a timid little mouse,
I squeak at my fear, which grows
Larger and larger.
My arch nemesis
The terror of terrors.

Holding the sword of death
Ready to strike me down in an evil blow.
Burning a fiery hole right through me.
I have no courage because my heart is scorched
Smoke wafting through the air.

My fear is the one
Watching from behind my back
With a shotgun under his arm.
When I turn around he is not there
But I know he is behind me taking aim.

My fear is black
But if I could turn
Look at my fear in the eye
And wield the axe of courage
I would strike it down.
Only then should I be able
To conquer my fear at last.

Matthew Pope (11)
Charters Ancaster College, Bexhill-on-Sea

Emotions

Fear
Cold, crisp snow
Icicles in dark corners
Daggers of hate bursting through your soul
Trickling whispers of terror
Your enemy of fate.

Love
A warm, toasty blanket
A hug, a smile, a care
Singled out achievements or a friend
A hand reaching out.
In your darkest hour.

Wonder
Problems waiting to be answered
Ticking clocks, chiming bells
A moment of thought
A hope
Questions?

Awe
The rising sun, a roaring wind
The blizzard howling.
Butterflies flapping enchanted wings
Or a still, clear pool of water
Changing, falling, rushing onwards
To a magnificent waterfall.

Katie Hatter (9)
Charters Ancaster College, Bexhill-on-Sea

Feelings

Happiness is all the colours of the rainbow
It tastes of juicy pineapple
Tingling my taste buds.
Smells like a field of sweet scented roses
Looks like a pot of gold
And sounds like trickling water
Dripping onto the cave floor.
Happiness is a big teddy, cuddling you close.

But sadness is dark and gloomy
The colour black.
It tastes of sour lemons forcing out your tears.
It looks like a bubbling cauldron of hate
And sounds like funeral bells
Clanging the sound of death.
Sadness is a deep pit, a crumbling wall
Crushing you to dust.

Rosie Reeve (11)
Charters Ancaster College, Bexhill-on-Sea

Underwater World

U nderwater world
N asty shark, the bloodthirsty king of the sea.
D olphins like rainbows, jumping up and down
E verything moving so fast.
R ubbery jellyfish with tentacles stinging
W hales, big and fearful sea monsters.
A   golden fish moving swiftly
T iny crabs scuttling craftily
E ncountering a wriggling snake
R apid waves washing from side to side.

Jack Kitchen (8)
Charters Ancaster College, Bexhill-on-Sea

Take Care!

Danger is a tiger
Fierce and sneaky
Brave and quick
Blending amongst the leaves
Waiting for its prey.
It sounds like a
Prolonged, shrill scream
And feels as sharp as a spear.

Fear is a snake
Shiny and smooth
Sliding in and out
Amongst the stones
Striking venom as it kills.
It sounds like a deafening shriek
And feels like
A frozen sheet of ice.

Emma Bignell (11)
Charters Ancaster College, Bexhill-on-Sea

The Wise Dragon

His tail is a sharp blade shining in the moonlight
His claws are like daggers
His scales glow
And his head is a range of colour.

When he breathes fire
It flashes out
In blistering red, yellow and orange.

He is swift and green and soars like an eagle
He is as long as a snake
And as quick as a cheetah.

Danny Horton (8)
Charters Ancaster College, Bexhill-on-Sea

Clickety Clack

Clickety, clickety clack, the train goes along the track,
Clickety, clickety clack, the train goes along the track.

Where it stops nobody knows
Only the driver knows where it goes.
It slows down going round a bend
Then comes to a halt as it reaches the end.

Clickety, clickety clack, the train goes along the track,
Clickety, clickety clack, the train goes along the track.

Then off it goes once again
Maybe it will pass a lane.
Stopping, it screeches; a terrible sound
And that terrible sound can be heard all around.

Clickety, clickety clack, the train goes along the track,
Clickety, clickety clack, the train goes along the track.

At last it bends around like a snake
Goes over a bridge and next to a lake.
It slows down going round a bend
Then it comes to a halt as it reaches the end.

Clickety, clickety clack, the train goes along the track,
Clickety, clickety clack, the train goes along the track.

Stephen Kennedy-Redmile-Gordon (9)
Charters Ancaster College, Bexhill-on-Sea

Spiders

One of the things I really hate
Are those horrid eight-legged spiders
Those terrible insect bloodsuckers
Those frightening little web-gliders.

The reason why I hate spiders so
Is because I have arachnophobia.

I hate . . .
Big ones
Little ones
Medium-sized ones
They are all a horrid memorabilia!

So next time you say:
'There's a spider!'
I will scream,
Shout
And bellow.

I will make every glass shatter.
You will see me a frightened white
Instead of a happy yellow!

Daisy Reece (10)
Charters Ancaster College, Bexhill-on-Sea

Anger

Like a volcano erupting
Fighting in a war
Red-hot air
With red-hot face
Fury slapping
Bricks falling
Unleashing anger.

Tristan King (7)
Fletching CE Primary School, Uckfield

Happiness

It sounds quiet as feet in the snow
It tastes like cotton candy following your footsteps in the snow
It smells like marshmallow coming from the baker with
                                     doughnut crumbs on top
It looks like red and pink love hearts, all around, love and happiness
It feels like a newborn kitten, two seconds after all of them all
                                                around you.

Brooke Sones (7)
Fletching CE Primary School, Uckfield

Sadness

Water dashing through rocks with a breeze
Going through trees with leaves rustling gently
Rushing clouds looking down at the sea
With patterns of the sunlight
Glittering, shining down
The sea crashing the cliffs
The tide coming onto the sand.

Christopher St Denis (8)
Fletching CE Primary School, Uckfield

Darkness

Sounds like rumbling thunder,
As cold as snow on a winter's night,
It smells like fear in the night,
It looks like a very dark tunnel with no end,
It feels very, very cold,
Like chocolate cake in a freezer.
It reminds me of being at the North Pole at midnight.

Philip Fletcher (7)
Fletching CE Primary School, Uckfield

Sadness

It sounds like the hooting of a night-time owl.
It tastes of cold ice cream on a cold and windy day.
It smells of snowflakes floating through the air.
It looks like the glittering trees dancing in the wind.
It feels like bits of snow floating onto your nose.
It reminds me of the waves crashing onto the cliff in a nice sort of way.

Maysie Coe (7)
Fletching CE Primary School, Uckfield

Darkness

Sounds like the rumble of thunder in a giant storm.
As cold as snow on a cold winter's night.
Smells like a dead deer left for a year.
As dark, as dark as an infinite tunnel.
It reminds me of the bitter pain the Israelites had within slavery.

Anna Roe (8)
Fletching CE Primary School, Uckfield

Anger

It sounds like when I scream when I'm hurt
It tastes like burnt marshmallow
It smells like burning wood
It looks like red lava
It feels like hot steam
It reminds me of being told what to do.

Lydia Bunyard (7)
Fletching CE Primary School, Uckfield

Maybe . . .

Around a tree
A hedgehog dives under
I always do wonder
What the world is like down there?

Maybe,
There are great long passageways
And storerooms
With tiny cupboards.

Maybe,
It's a door to another world
With shops
And even cinemas!

Maybe,
It could just be
A big pile of leaves
That smell really bad!

Maybe,
That could be true,
But that would be no fun,
You've got to have some imagination . . .

Anne Cole (11)
Great Ballard School, Chichester

The Sky And The Sea

In the clouded sky
Where the birds reign all above
(Well except the ostrich)
With the peace-keeping dove.

The dark blue sea
Hides many creatures
Among its coral features
But still we spoil the sea with pollution.

Sam Terry (10)
Great Ballard School, Chichester

Winter - Cold Or Warm?

For more than one reason,
Winter is an unusual season.
The swallows migrate
And hedgehogs hibernate.

Trees have lost their leaves,
Their branches are bare.
There most certainly is
A chill in the air.

Families and friends,
Around the tree together.
Does anybody notice,
Cold or warm weather?

Hayley Mackay (10)
Great Ballard School, Chichester

On The Moor

On the moor
The willow weeps
Plant roots seep
Down to the deep.

The thistles thrive
The fish are alive
The kingfisher dives
The tadpoles strive.

In the dark
Came a dog that did bark
Left its mark
And woke the skylark.

Oliver Coombe-Tennant (10)
Great Ballard School, Chichester

Hedgehog

In the main I like being a hedgehog
But sometimes it's a pain.

As I waddle along the forest floor,
I trip and stumble and then I fall.
I never have the time to rest,
In case I don't look my best.

It's always a bad hair day,
Whether it's March or May.
And finally, as I curl up tight
I tumble then get a fright
And waddle right away again.

Waddle in,
Waddle out,
Waddle, waddle all about.

Clara Butterworth (10)
Great Ballard School, Chichester

Nature

As I tread through the woods, silent and cold
I hear noises like a crunch
From the floor below.

My knees are trembling
So I go and sit down under a tree
Where the leaves are damp.

I hear shooting in the distance
When the birds fly up
I hear voices all around me
So I jump up.

Amelia Pickles (10)
Great Ballard School, Chichester

My Teacher Is An Alien!

Every night Professor Zodiac takes off his face
And tries to communicate with outer space.
His skin is green
It makes me scream.

He has three eyes,
Which is no surprise.
He's got a pet germ
That's the size of a worm.

I don't have a clue what junk he eats
Probably a piece of human meat.
He has an alien girlfriend too
Sometimes she acts like a monkey
From the local zoo.

Thank goodness Professor Zodiac is retiring soon,
Hopefully he'll fly right back to the moon.

Jessica Simmonds (10)
Great Ballard School, Chichester

In The Night

In the night I heard a very scary noise,
It sounded like someone was playing with my toys,
I got out of my bed to see,
What that scary noise could really be,
I checked the whole house
And there it was; a little furry mouse,
I decided to go back to bed,
Because there was a really big pain in my head.

Elisa Castro (10)
Great Ballard School, Chichester

My Best Friend

My best friend called Jess,
Doesn't really like playing chess.
She's got long, brown hair,
We really do make a pair.

We are in the football team
All I do is scream and scream,
'Come on Jess you can do it,
Watch yourself you're gonna get hit!'

Now I'll tell you about my best friend's style,
It really is quite a pile.
Well, she likes to shop
And she never stops.
So that's why I like her 'cause she's bonkers,
That's why she's my best friend!

Ysabelle Shopland (11)
Great Ballard School, Chichester

Ten Things Found In A Witch's Pocket . . .

A bottle of eye of newt
An amazing stew of frogs' legs and eyes
An acrobatic bottle of flies
An expensive bottle of champagne
A social worker called Elaine
A bottle of death potion
A CD called 'Death with Emotion'
A poison berry
A humungous ferry
And a bird's breath.

Etienne Robinson-Sivyer (8)
Hellingly CP School, Hailsham

As I Looked Over My Garden Wall

As I look over my garden wall, I see the terror it does install.
As a war is going on and innocent people are in the brawl.
Kids doing crime, thinking it's cool,
But it's just nonsense, that is its all.
Violence is catching on in a haze,
Just like the human race, taking a colossal pace.
What is this world coming to?
Kind people dying, though nothing they can do.
Violence is from badness, nowhere it should belong.
I wish it could be gone.
Nations dropping bombs, badness filling the brains of innocent ones.
Ongoing suffering like a train going alone.
People addicted to drugs, they are consequently taking.
People aren't giving, it's more that's being taken.
Poor ones are baking, unsheltered in the sun,
Some with no food, they don't know what's going on.
People go to work to get pay, to live a standard life every day.
Then look at me. Living a life of luxury.
I see a gang, beating up a black man.
Racism is to blame. The world should hang its head in shame.
And why were guns invented? Shooting people's livers.
All it does it send a shiver running up my spine.
I wish the world could be mine.
But I wouldn't punish the criminals,
I would help them change their ways.
If I didn't, I would be like them.
All I want is a peaceful world,
One with love,
That is all.

Jack Moloney (11)
Hellingly CP School, Hailsham

River Poem

Crystal clear water, rippling along
Golden water lilies
Floating past
Oars splashing
In and out
Of the water.

It sparkles
Like jewels
Soon it roars like a
Monster
As it races along
Bubbling and spurting
As it flows out of a spring.

The river turns from
Crystal clear
To muddy brown
Big green bottles
And logs
Chucked in selfishly
The river is spoilt.

At last the river
Reaches the sea
Seagulls squawk overhead
Crabs scuttle in and out
Of the sea
The river ends here.

Lucy Egleton (9)
Jessie Younghusband Primary School, Chichester

The Red Dragon - Haiku

Bang, bang on the drums
The beautiful red dragon
Scared the beast away.

Andrew Main (11)
Jessie Younghusband Primary School, Chichester

A Cautionary Tale

Once there was a boy called Gregg
For food he would always beg and beg
One morning Gregg ate so much
He polished off a massive lunch.

He ate a whole chocolate cake
Five sausages, a ketchup lake
Both of the greasy chicken legs
And 10 enormous scrambled eggs.

After that he was terribly ill
He took an overdose of pills
The doctor came and looked amazed
He said that Gregg was extremely dazed.

He said that Gregg would soon be dead
Because he was far too overfed
Just then Gregg's heart suddenly stopped
And at that moment he horribly popped.

Douglas Morrison (10)
Jessie Younghusband Primary School, Chichester

Friend - Haiku

A chocolate-sweet smile
Laughter rippling over her
Caring, playing friend.

Olivia Whatmore (10)
Jessie Younghusband Primary School, Chichester

Footie Coming Home - Haiku

The odds are well on
For England to beat Holland
Because of Rooney.

Samuel Peake (10)
Jessie Younghusband Primary School, Chichester

Autumn Wind

The drizzly rain howls at
The sun to go away
Because autumn's begun.

A handful of leaves
Fall from the sky
As if a giant has passed by.

But autumn vanishes
When winter is near
It's time to say goodbye
And I'll see you
Next year.

Joy Horton (10)
Jessie Younghusband Primary School, Chichester

Tanka

Chinese banquet waits,
Noodles slick and slimy too,
Rice waits just for you,
Prawn crackers have quite a price,
But I suppose they're quite nice!

Harriet Smith (10)
Jessie Younghusband Primary School, Chichester

Haiku

Fireworks red and blue
Dragons dancing through the streets
Beautiful colours.

Rosie Little (11)
Jessie Younghusband Primary School, Chichester

Winter Wind

The winter wind is icily cold
Mean and vicious, brave and bold.
It howls and bawls, groans and roars
Grunting like a herd of boars.

Causes screaming down the street
Wrecking trees and blowing sheets.
The winter wind is the strongest one,
It doesn't halt until it's won!

Toby White (9)
Jessie Younghusband Primary School, Chichester

Sir Francis Drake

Sir Francis will sail out to sea
Great, oh great, so mighty is he.
He also sailed the Channel too
He sailed across the sea, bright blue.
He had a brave and mighty crew
It got cold and he turned quite blue.
When the Spanish came out to sea
He sprang right up, how can that be?

Rebecca Harrington (8)
Jessie Younghusband Primary School, Chichester

Summer Wind

The wind is smooth but painfully hot,
The heat is dangerous,
The steamy-hot wind is baking my skull,
The scorching sun's wind is hitting my thighs,
Sending me inside.

Reuben Underhill (10)
Jessie Younghusband Primary School, Chichester

The Well

The silent thoughts of the well,
Fill up your empty space,
It fills up with joy and happiness,
As you admire the peacefulness of its wooden depths.

Your mind drifts away,
As you look deep down at the colourful stones,
You can see your face appear,
In the patterns of the rock.

The bright sun bounces off the wooden seats,
I'm in a world of my own,
No worries -
Only memories.

Megan Gent (9)
Jessie Younghusband Primary School, Chichester

The School Grounds

I can see everything
In the shade and in the sun
I feel like I'm free
For once, I feel like me.

The birds overhead -
I hear them rushing by
It will be long before I die
But now it feels so soon.

I smell the scent of flowers
I could stay here for hours
Sitting on the mounds -
I can see all the school grounds.

Chloe Sellwood (10)
Jessie Younghusband Primary School, Chichester

River Poem

The river chases through the valley
Like a car racing in a rally.
Showers of rocks falling in the river,
The thought of falling in is a shiver!
Rocks smoothed down to pebbles,
People cheering as winners get their medals,
The river calms down as it reaches flat land,
The river is dreaming about the country of sand.
The river now carries a small boat,
Swans and other waterfowl are afloat,
The river now enters saltwater,
Flooding into its big delta,
The river now enters the sea,
The water has no chance to flee.

Andrew Creswick (9)
Jessie Younghusband Primary School, Chichester

Come To Our School

Jessie school is somewhere I think,
We do lots of lessons that link,
We have friends that play on the mounds,
While our parents go shopping in towns.

We change our books in reading time,
Then it's lunchtime and we eat lime,
We get star awards from the head
And we used to write in black lead.

Katie Adams (8)
Jessie Younghusband Primary School, Chichester

Tudor Haikus

Red, yellow and white
The Tudor rose made pretty
To represent fights.

A great big palace
Some proud standing entrance gates
Hampton Court's royal.

All of Henry's wives,
Two divorced, two beheaded
Another survived.

Abbey Lamb (8)
Jessie Younghusband Primary School, Chichester

School Haikus

Our school is the best
The uniform's dark black, blue
We are courteous.

We have a playground
A trim trail and equipment
Peaceful area.

Friends are the greatest
Play with hoops and bouncy balls
On the trim trail wall.

Georgina Warner (8)
Jessie Younghusband Primary School, Chichester

Tudor Haikus

Big and horrible
Eats for his life every day
Runs and falls over.

Proud, rich and happy
Earrings brought from far away
Then he had enough.

Henry the VIII fights,
The Mary Rose is with him,
Fast away he goes.

Octavia Musumeci (9)
Jessie Younghusband Primary School, Chichester

Tudor Haikus

Henry haunts the room
The smell of cloves follows him
His footsteps echo.

The six wives grumble
Invent the apple crumble
Our tummies rumble.

Hannah New (9)
Jessie Younghusband Primary School, Chichester

What Is Love?

Love is pink like candyfloss hearts
Love is white like a sparkling jewel
Love is blue like a hot summer's day
Love is red like a beautiful flower.

Charlotte Russell (7)
Little Common School, Bexhill-on-Sea

Art

Art can be a variety of things
Some people use their imagination
But with others . . .
It just leads to frustration.

Different people use different colours,
Some are light,
Some are dark,
Some giving people quite a fright.

There's just one thing,
People usually have the same,
Nearly everyone always draws a picture,
But it doesn't always lead to fame.

Poppy Lelliott (9)
Little Common School, Bexhill-on-Sea

Classroom Poem

C lassrooms are full of children
L earning
A ll sorts of subjects
S ome classes are smart and
S ome are untidy, but
R eally most are working hard
O ften the classrooms are noisy
O ccasionally they are quiet
M ostly pupils are well behaved
S o the school is a better place.

Elliott Leonard-Diss (9)
Little Common School, Bexhill-on-Sea

School Time

S nacks and fruit on the playground
C ounting numbers in maths sets
H oping that playtime will come soon
O pening the doors to the small hall and
O pening the doors for visitors and teachers
L ittle Common School is a great school

T ime to go home now
I can't wait for tomorrow
M aking lovely pictures
E ven painting our own buildings.

Fern Denney (9)
Little Common School, Bexhill-on-Sea

Mathematics

M ixing numbers into sums
A dding is a mind teaser
T here are three sorts of triangles
H exagons are a six-sided shape
E ven adding is hard
M ultiplying is
A mind twister
T ime is quick
I n a
C ats test
S ubtracting is a brain bender.

George Stinson (9)
Little Common School, Bexhill-on-Sea

Happiness

H appiness fills the world with joy
A ccept the offers from your friends to play
P ick up the happiness from your friends and give it to other people
P ick up the invitation and go
I love happiness
N ever be angry
E verywhere will be happiness
S pread happiness everywhere
S easons will make you happy!

William Templeton (7)
Little Common School, Bexhill-on-Sea

Sunset

Sunset is a wonderful time just before it gets dark,
It has a heart-warming silence and everyone is leaving the park
It has beautiful and delightful colours
The most lovely thing you would see
Just like the prettiest autumn leaves.

Azjad Elmubarak (8)
Little Common School, Bexhill-on-Sea

Friends

Friends will be nice, very nice to you
Friends take you to their houses
Friends give you ice cream
Friends give you presents.

Ellis Evento (7)
Little Common School, Bexhill-on-Sea

Playground

P eople playing with their friends
L eaning on the walls and wriggly bends
A acting out lots of different games
Y elling to each other and playing football with James
G etting caught while playing it
R unning round keeps you fit
O f all the games I like to play
U nderneath the climbing frame, it is today
N othing compares to being around
D ancing and singing in our fantastic *playground!*

Harry Saville (9)
Little Common School, Bexhill-on-Sea

Subjects

S cience you must learn
U nderstanding is the keyword here
B e a fighter with your work
J ust go that one step further
E nglish
C omputer room
T ests
S o much I can't fit in, but school just
    drifts you into another world.

Matthew Edwards (9)
Little Common School, Bexhill-on-Sea

Love Is . . .

Love is blue like a river
Love is white like a dove
Love is red like rubies
Love is green like fresh grass.

Alexander Christodoulou (7)
Little Common School, Bexhill-on-Sea

Teachers

This poem is all about teachers, so you better watch out,
Teachers always wonder why we all start snoring
Probably because some lessons are so, so boring
Why can't we teach the teachers?
Well, if we told them off they would turn into *screechers!*
Never go behind a teacher who has a counting stick,
'Cause if she turns around, boy you've got to be quick
I hope you take this in mind, because you could find
If you do the opposite of what I've said
The teachers will end up *shaving your head!*

Jack Taylor (10)
Little Common School, Bexhill-on-Sea

Winter

W ind whistling through the trees
 I cicles drooping from frozen branches
N ight-time long and dark
T yphoons swirling around the world
E ating English breakfast
R ivers iced over.

Ben Profit (10)
Little Common School, Bexhill-on-Sea

Spring Flowers Blooming

The wind was blowing, the rain was pouring
And the spring flowers were blooming.
Oh how my heart was pounding
When the park keeper swept all the leaves away!
On this rainbow sort of day.

Toni Cearns (7)
Little Common School, Bexhill-on-Sea

Playground Fun

P laying in the playground lots, of fun and glee
L earning is now over, come run around with me
A ction is all around me
Y oung children are all laughing, so much fun and joy
G ames are all so much fun, people playing with toys
R ound and round they all run, most of them are boys
O utside is my favourite place to play
U nder the sky we will play on the playground today
N othing will stop us having fun
D ancing and skipping all around the playground

F unny games, jokes and toys, lots of fun for everyone
U nfortunately play is over and it's at an end
N ow the teachers will pack away and home we will get sent!

Lewis Kemp (9)
Little Common School, Bexhill-on-Sea

Lovely Butterflies

Butterflies glow through the bright blue light, so lovely to see
You must watch them fly through the moonlight to their bright red bed
Flying in the daylight to the bright pink and purple flowers
Do you like butterflies?
I do.

Sonya Sharma (7)
Little Common School, Bexhill-on-Sea

Love

Love is orange like a flaming hot day
Love is white like a precious dove
Love is red like a volcano blazing
Love is green like fresh grass.

Sam Hodger (8)
Little Common School, Bexhill-on-Sea

I've Got To Get There First!

I've got to get the gold
Because last year I came third
It's nearly my turn to race
So my wheel better not hit the kerb
This time round the circuit
I better not crash and burn it.

The pistol is about to be fired,
I'm ready and wired,
Bang!
The gun's gone off,
I'm accelerating hard, round the circuit I charge,
My wheels are spinning left and right as I navigate in the light.

I can see the finish line
This is going to be my best lap time
Oh yes, I've won the race
Now I can be presented first place
No more worrying about third place
Because I'm the Rally Champion!

Oscar Hammond (9)
Little Common School, Bexhill-on-Sea

My Footie

I love my football day
It is on a Saturday
I do not know what I would do
If I could not have my football today.

I love to play in goal
But I don't always get a chance
I expect I will be a defender
Ryan will be a midfielder.

We will have a great game I know
Plenty of goals to show
Then have to wait a week
For my favourite football day.

Samuel Hills (10)
Little Common School, Bexhill-on-Sea

The Solar System

T he solar system is very vast
H urry through the asteroid belt, as
E arth is moving very fast

S o, rocket through the atmosphere
O ver the moon and past the stars
L ook left and right, see Jupiter
A nd Neptune, Venus, Pluto and Mars
R eturn a little and you will find

S aturn with its fiery halos
Y es, we mustn't forget Uranus
S o, we have now travelled the solar system
T o learn about the world we're in. Hope you've
E njoyed our little tour and hopefully one day life will be found on
M ars!

Liam Berriman (9)
Little Common School, Bexhill-on-Sea

School Time

Six hours a day we go to school
We have assemblies in the small hall.
Sometimes we have spellings, sometimes we have art
The teachers at our school are very, very smart.

Children run around and yell all day
After school they come round and play.
We love to sing, we love to dance
And put on plays when we get the chance.

Every day wo do our best
Just in case we havo a test.
Our trampling feet rattle the glass
As we run out the class.

Alice Geraghty (9)
Little Common School, Bexhill-on-Sea

Mother Nature

The birds and the bees
All play music in the breeze
The rain and the snow
The frost will freeze
Mother Nature is all around
What you see and every sound.

The sun and the sea
Is so good for me
The wind and the tide
To take a stroll beside
Mother Nature is all around
What you see and every sound.

Jonathan Corke (10)
Little Common School, Bexhill-on-Sea

Lessons

English
Crazy commas
Loony letters
Super stories
Wacky writing

Maths
Supreme sums
Freaky fractions
Ambitious angles
Tricky time

PE
Violent volleyball
Seasonal swimming
Dainty dancing
Gentle gym.

Georgia Lea (9)
Little Common School, Bexhill-on-Sea

Under The Sea

Under the sea
Is where I want to be
I see lots of fish
Quite a tasty dish.

Round the volcanoes dark
Beware of sharks
Sunken ships
Filled with bodies and hips.

It's a wonderful sight,
Colours both dark and bright
Along the bottom I creep
So very, very deep.

The coral so rare
We need to take care
Or before too long
It'll all be gone.

Let's all be aware
That we take good care
Of the wonderful life we see
Under the sea.

Matthew Middleton (9)
Little Common School, Bexhill-on-Sea

Nature

The bright blue sky like a deep blue sea
the sun looks like a flower with burnt orange and yellow petals
the luscious green grass like a forest with the wind blowing in your face
like a cheetah running
old ladies' wrinkles like twisted tree roots in an enchanted forest
for many hundreds of years.

George Jeffery (9)
Little Common School, Bexhill-on-Sea

World War I

Down on the battlefield, the weary soldiers fight with rifles in
                                                       their hands,
Scrambling out of the trenches storming the enemy with
                                                       surprise attacks.
When one man falls down, another helps him back to the trenches
                                                       for medical attention.
Behind the trenches the nurses treat the wounded in safety,
While the unwounded carry on the hard fight.
In the background artillery and anti aircraft guns boom,
Their noise echoing around.
Then 11 o'clock comes and all falls silent,
For it is the eleventh of November 1918.

Jack Roadway (9)
Little Common School, Bexhill-on-Sea

Winter

W ild storms rage roughly
 I ncreasing power every second
N ever to stop
T errorising buildings and animals
E veryone is scared
R ecklessly rushing through the land.

Cameron Kirk (10)
Little Common School, Bexhill-on-Sea

Deep Blue Sea

Waves swish up and down in the shape of a smile and a frown.
Under the rock pool pebbles and shells and slimy sea snails
Horses galloping in the sea where the fish make their tea
When it's time to go to sleep, the fish will never peep.

Danielle Sellers (9)
Little Common School, Bexhill-on-Sea

Lily My Dog

L oving with no one to spare
I ncredibly beautiful beagle
L ying in sunshine just there
Y oung and very bouncy

M ysterious about the world
Y elping at the door

D igging her treasure intensely
O bedient with food much more
G entle and cheerful my pup.

Jack Vincent (10)
Little Common School, Bexhill-on-Sea

Happiness

H appiness is when you have a smile on your face
A t a party you have a fun time
P ick your best toy and ask if you can buy it, you'll be happy
P ick up the happiness from your friend
I spread happiness to my friends
N ice when you spread happiness
E at stuff that makes you feel happy
S pread your happiness all over the world
S ell unhappiness and buy happiness!

Darragh Groves (7)
Little Common School, Bexhill-on-Sea

Smile On Your Birthday

Smile on your birthday to bring
good thoughts, smile on your
birthday to make people
happy, smile on your birthday
and appreciate your present.

Katie Moore (9)
Little Common School, Bexhill-on-Sea

My Little Dog Clifford

My little dog Clifford is quite a scamp
My mum and dad call him a tramp.

He chases the birds up into the trees
But he can't even jump up to my knees.

He barks and runs around the trees
And he still can't even jump to my knees.

He is lots of fun and come what may
After school he makes my day.

Jazer Barclay (10)
Little Common School, Bexhill-on-Sea

The Dragon

The big, red dragon with pointed wings
Lived in a cave with lots of things
He was fat and ugly and smiled very smugly
When Prince Charming came
He came to save his mum
He killed the dragon
Dead!

Joshua Eaton (9)
Little Common School, Bexhill-on-Sea

Eeyore

Eeyore is a sweet donkey,
Nothing can stop him being that
And I'm going to love him
Forever and that's that!

Abbie Latasha Beale (9)
Little Common School, Bexhill-on-Sea

This Monster

This monster landed on Earth,
He had big eyes and big green spots.
He had four arms and six legs,
His body was covered in Jelly Tots.

This monster landed on Earth
And crashed down five buildings.
He was seven feet tall and weighed a tonne,
Broke into a jewellery shop and stole some rings.

Now this monster decided to leave
And go back to the place he came from.
The monster got back in his ship
To go back to planet Sentom.

This monster landed on Earth one day,
'Will you offer me a place to stay?'

Cameron Smith (10)
Little Common School, Bexhill-on-Sea

When I Was Little

When I was little
I was a bit of a pickle
I used to kick and scream
But when I was good
I was a dream.

When I was little
My big sister loved to hold me
We would splash in the sea
Eat lots of ice cream
When I was little
This is how it used to be.

Lydia Luck (9)
Little Common School, Bexhill-on-Sea

Naomi Got Stuck

Naomi is a silly girl,
Who is accident-prone,
It's best to keep away from her
And leave her well alone.

Naomi got her finger stuck,
In her purse,
She went to hospital
And was treated by a nurse.

Naomi got her foot stuck,
In a cereal packet,
She tried to get it off again,
But was caught up in her jacket.

Naomi got her bottom stuck,
On a car,
When the driver got in it,
He drove Naomi far.

Naomi got her body stuck,
In a shark's tooth trap,
She struggled all over the place,
But sharky went . . .
Snap!

Andrew Slinn (9)
Little Common School, Bexhill-on-Sea

Sometimes

Sometimes I'm clever,
Sometimes I'm sad,
Sometimes I'm good,
Sometimes I'm bad,
Sometimes I'm helpful
And help cook the tea,
But mostly I'm just me!

Jodie Boyle (9)
Little Common School, Bexhill-on-Sea

Cheeky Boy

Out of the window the old lady looks
Watching the world go by.

Often I look up at her sitting there
It makes me wonder why?

She turns her head, her eyes don't move
Is she looking at me?

I look around, there's no one else
Except a dog and tree.

It's me for sure she's looking at
Are my flies undone?

I'll have to check, no they are not
So I poke out my tongue.

Callum Hall (9)
Little Common School, Bexhill-on-Sea

My Dog Wilf
(Ode to a Westie)

Wilf is our dog, his legs are small
Recently we took him for walks and he took a fall
Now he limps about
With a sad looking snout

O' Wilf O' Wilf the vet will sort you out!
O' Wilf O' Wilf the vet will sort you out!

He's three years old and too young for a stick,
Unless it's the sort you throw and he licks!

O' Wilf O' Wilf the vet will sort you out!
O' Wilf O' Wilf the vet will sort you out!

Toby Cowling (10)
Little Common School, Bexhill-on-Sea

Happiness

H appiness is green like skipping in the meadow
A nimals white like fluffy little clouds
P eople are like monkeys hanging onto trees
P olar bears are like soft white cushions on your bed
I ce is cold like ice cream
N ever get sad, think happy all the time
E verybody be happy all day long
S and is like the yellow sun
S and gets in your toes, yummy!

Emma Jeffery (7)
Little Common School, Bexhill-on-Sea

School

School is great
School is fun
School is here for everyone

I go to school every day
I play with my mates
It is great

When the bell rings at nine
It's time for us to sit down and shine
We work hard all day to deserve our play.

Luke Whiting (10)
Little Common School, Bexhill-on-Sea

Happiness

Happiness makes me jolly.
Happiness makes me smile.
Happiness makes me wink.
Happiness makes me have a nice day!

Lydia Harrison (7)
Little Common School, Bexhill-on-Sea

Germs

Germs are crawling on me and you
And sometimes crawling out the loo
All waiting in an armour suit
Some germs shouting 'Toot toot,'
And they all hop inside your bed!
And hold on to your favourite ted!

Germs are not able to see
So don't you start staring at me
You won't be able to see one on me so stop it
But if you wriggle about to and fro you might be able to drop it!
(But whatever you do don't let one get on *me!)*

Milly Clifford (9)
Little Common School, Bexhill-on-Sea

Maths

M aths is very fun
A nd cool too
T eachers are good at maths
    Our teacher is called Mr Lion
H e is very kind to us and he is
S uch good fun.

Ben Stiles (9)
Little Common School, Bexhill-on-Sea

Winter Poem

Winter sounds like rain crashing to the ground like a stone.
Winter sounds like icebergs crashing together.
Winter feels like a frozen snowflake settling on my back.
Winter is time to play, no more time to climb the hay.
This is what I believe,
When I snuggle up in a deep sleep.

Dominic Henry (9)
Milton Mount Primary School, Crawley

Please Help Me

I miss my mum, I miss my dad,
They sent me away 'cause I was bad,
When I saw the world away from home,
I was isolated, I was sad, now I'm all on my own.
I wish they would forgive me when I say sorry,
But they sent me away in the back of a lorry.
Now I know how bad it is to do wrong,
I wish I was at home where I belong.
But I'm all on my own and I have no home,
Please help me . . .
Somebody.

Natalie Bale (11)
Milton Mount Primary School, Crawley

The Wild Horse

Galloping over fences,
Hardly touching the ground,
The wild horse is jumping
And doesn't make a sound.

Grazing on green grass,
Bending his head down low,
Then bringing it up swiftly
And swaying it to and fro.

Proudly he will stand,
Watching over his distant herd,
Then cantering to meet them,
As swiftly as a bird.

Now that night has come
And everything is black,
Our beautiful horse shall sleep,
Until morning comes back.

Rebecca Bala (10)
Milton Mount Primary School, Crawley

Arsenal Rock!

There he goes, back and forth,
Here he runs, south and north.
In the footie match, he shoots and scores,
Everywhere there's a round of applause.
Robert Pires, he is good,
Dribbling down as he should.
He passes the ball to Ashley Cole,
Oh yeah! What a goal!
There goes Ljungberg taking a corner,
There goes Campbell tripping over,
We all know David Seaman's left,
He was a goalkeeper, one of the best!

Masuma Shamsi (11)
Milton Mount Primary School, Crawley

Cats And Dogs

Dogs always jump around
And make a funny sound.
They bark all day
And always want to play.
When you hear them walk around,
It makes you want to shout aloud.
They always lick you to death,
And never take a single breath,
That's why dogs are the best.

Cats like to have a cuddle,
But sometimes get in a muddle.
They like to play
And sometimes catch prey
They jump up and down
And love to be around,
That's why they're so cute.

Chelsey Wells (11)
Milton Mount Primary School, Crawley

My Football Idol Is Andy Johnson!

Johnson is the best!
Better than the rest!
He's in the England squad!
His boots never clod!
He's like thunder on the ground,
Zooming all around!
He sounds like David Beckham!
He scores like he's in Heaven!
My dad supports Palace too!
They're the Eagles! Woohoo!
To keep fit, he doesn't eat chips!
Crystal Palace are in the Premiership!
They're out of the FA Cup, but I don't care
Because they are the best! Oh yeah!

Luke Knight (11)
Milton Mount Primary School, Crawley

Seasons

In spring, the flowers begin to bloom
'Cause they know summer is coming soon.
Leaves on trees begin to grow,
Grass is growing, soon to mow.

In summer the sun shines hot,
We sail again on our yacht.
The warm winds are light,
Oh what a pretty sight.

In autumn the leaves begin to fall,
Colder days for one and all.
The birds begin to fly away
To warmer places far away.

In winter the cold wind blows,
Sometimes it even snows.
The roads can be covered in ice,
But sitting round our fire is nice.

Grant Bevis (10)
Milton Mount Primary School, Crawley

I Live Alone On An Island

I don't remember very much.

L ong have I waited for someone to touch.
I may be left behind,
V ery strong storms may have occurred,
E ven if I never heard.

A m I left behind?
L onely I start to feel, someone come to me now.
O h how the breeze seems to torment me.
N ow I feel left behind,
E ating alone on a sandy trail.

O n and on the days pass,
N o one for me to grasp.

A nd how long will I feel left behind?
N ever a break from my heartache.

I walk on hot sand and leave my print,
S o sweetly the seagulls sing.
L uxurious water can soothe my feet,
A nd as time goes on, the island will shrink.
N ow I wonder, am I left behind?
D on't leave me, it's too late to say.

Kimali Brook (11)
Milton Mount Primary School, Crawley

Holidays

H olidays are the best,
O h it's a good time to rest.
I aying on a nice hot beach,
I t must take a long time to reach.
D ays at school are boring,
A nd holidays are roaring.
Y ou go to different places each time,
S ometimes you can eat lime.

Kiran Sajjan (11)
Milton Mount Primary School, Crawley

I Would Like To . . .

I would like to touch the moon and grow a chocolate tree.
I would like to cuddle a cloud and talk to a star.
I would like to feel the purr of a cat and touch a lion.
I would like to hear the monkeys chattering.

I would like to have an everlasting gobstopper.
I would like my kitten to talk to me and come to school.
I would like to do a proper handstand,
Walk on a rainbow and see the grass grow.

I would like a butterfly to sit on my finger.
I would like to swim in the sea with dolphins.
I would like to dig a burrow with my bunny.
I would like to sit on top of the world and escape to Mars.

Alice Lloyd (7)
Milton Mount Primary School, Crawley

Seasons Galore

The sun starts to shine,
The flowers start opening,
Here comes the springtime.

The sun shines brightly.
Sitting in the golden sand,
Here comes the summer.

Crispy leaves fall down,
The weather starts to cool down,
Here comes the autumn.

Frosty, white snowflakes
In a winter wonderland,
Here comes the winter.

Winter, summer, spring
And autumn, all the seasons
In seasons galore.

Jessica Davison (11)
Milton Mount Primary School, Crawley

Seasons

Springtime is fun,
From the clouds appears the sun.
The flowers are growing,
Their colours are also glowing.

Summertime is bright,
There is no sign of fright.
The sun is shining,
The whole world is smiling.

Autumn time is sad,
It makes you flipping mad.
The flowers are going,
There's no sign of colours showing.

Wintertime is cold,
The snow runs through your fingers like gold.
Freezing, icy snow,
Be careful if you know.

Charlotte Cook (11)
Milton Mount Primary School, Crawley

I Would Like To . . .

I would like to touch the white clouds in the sky,
I would like to slide on the colourful rainbow,
I would like to fly in the air with the birds.

I would like to smell the deep smell of roses,
I would like to ride on a bird's back into the sky,
I would like to walk on the moon.

I would like to have powers to help people who are in danger,
I would like to eat the biggest chocolate cake,
I would like to see the petals on a flower open.

Ella Marsh (7)
Milton Mount Primary School, Crawley

A Winter's Day

Winter smells like a bitterly cold evening out.
Winter feels like you have frostbite all the time.
Winter looks like white all over the ground, under everyone's feet
　　　　　　　　　　　while they're running about.
Winter reminds me of icicles in caves and going skiing
And snowboarding on mountains.

Kieran Fellows (10)
Milton Mount Primary School, Crawley

On A Winter's Night

Winter sounds like ice skates slashing,
Meanwhile, icicles are dripping.
Winter feels like frosty snowflakes
Falling down, down to the ground.
Winter tastes like a snowball
Smashed into your face.
Winter smells like my brown, brown cocoa.
Winter reminds me of my family
Coming round and celebrating.

Georgia Davis (9)
Milton Mount Primary School, Crawley

Winter Is . . .

Winter sounds like icicles falling from the icy igloo.
Winter feels like being all warm and cosy,
With the heating on in the evening and morning too.
Winter tastes like hot turkey from the oven.
Winter smells like freezing frost from the garden.
Winter looks dull and white all the time.
Winter reminds me of holidays and Christmas,
Which are fun times of the year and are always near!

Adele Morris (10)
Milton Mount Primary School, Crawley

Winter, Winter Everywhere

Winter sounds like snow hitting the windows on a cold winter's
Dull night while waiting for a pile of presents.
Winter feels all cold and frosty.
Winter tastes like turkey and roast dinners on Christmas Day.
Winter smells like fresh snowflakes falling from the sky.
Winter looks like snow landing on the frosty grass.
Winter reminds me of Christmas and opening presents
With your friends and family.

Alexandra Karagoz (10)
Milton Mount Primary School, Crawley

Snowy

Winter sounds like droplets of rain splashing in a puddle.
Winter feels like ice-cold stones.
Winter tastes like cold water.
Winter looks like a bowl of frozen water.
Winter smells like a cold, frosty night.
Winter reminds me of ice cream.

Lee Marsh (10)
Milton Mount Primary School, Crawley

My Winter Poem

Winter sounds like the crashing of enormous icebergs
Winter feels bitter cold as the wind blows, blows and blows
Winter tastes like vanilla ice cream on a bright sunny day
Winter smells like cold icicles melting into a stream of spring water
Winter looks like a snowy scene from the ebony window
Winter reminds me of last year's frosty white snow.

Sivalekha Viramuthu (9)
Milton Mount Primary School, Crawley

My Poem

I would like to feel the moon in the night.
I want to feel how shiny a star is.
I would like to feel the sound of a helicopter as it soars through the air.
I would like to feel the smell of fresh bread baking
And crawl inside a giant grape to feel how juicy it is.

I would like to hear the leaves falling off trees.
I would like to hear a daisy grow.
I would like to hear a planet turn
And see what the planets are made of.
I would like to hear a cheese that talks
And I would like to hear the rain when it's falling from the sky.

I would like to taste the rainbow and imagine it's a rose.
I would like to taste the whistling of birds.
I would like to taste the fresh smell of doughnuts.
I'd like to taste the warmth of the sun
And taste the softness of a teddy bear.

I would like to ride on a pretty sunset, while watching the whales play.
I would like to ride on a feather that floats from the sky.
I want to ride on the moon.
I would like to ride on a snowflake
And ride on a goose's back.

I would like to get rid of all the fights.
I would like to spin a cloud to make a jumper
And sneak into a rabbit's hole.
I would like to see God
And ask Him what He thinks of the world.

Eleanor Terry (8)
Milton Mount Primary School, Crawley

Winter Monday Haiku

Cold, cold all around
Snowing on a winter's day
On a dank Monday.

Amy Froshaug (10)
Milton Mount Primary School, Crawley

I Would Like . . .

I would like to ride on a snowflake
And have a snowball fight with a snowman.
I would like to swim with mermaids
And ask the clams to show me their pearls.

I would like to ride a magical unicorn
And slide down its back to the tip of its tail.
I would like to become a dolphin
And sing along with the whales.

I would like to taste the rainbow
And smell the colour purple.
I would like to twinkle like a star
And take a bite out of the cheesy moon.

I would like to hold hands with an angel
And float away in the sky.
I would like to ride on a dragon's back
And smell its fiery breath.

Georgia Amos (7)
Milton Mount Primary School, Crawley

The Magic Box
(Based on 'Magic Box' by Kit Wright)

I will put in the box . . .
The coldness of a snow-white polar bear,
The bossiness of my siblings
And the scent of a fresh green plant.

I will put in the box . . .
The moon and the wind,
The colours of the rainbow
And the first cry of a baby.

My box is fashioned from lava, ashes and sapphire,
With darkness on the lid
And spells in the corners,
Its hinges are as sharp as lions' teeth.

Bradley Bell (7)
Milton Mount Primary School, Crawley

My Pets

My pets are so great.
Hamsters, cats, guinea pigs and more.
They are all my mates.
Moving quickly on the floor.
Whoops, they ran out of the door!

Running so, so quick.
Me and my family chase.
Fellas that are slick.
It is almost like a race.
We're behind in second place.

My cat is so fast.
Dodging in and out of trees.
Landscapes going past.
To run fast she bends her knees.
Eventually we go home.

Alexander Lamm (10)
Milton Mount Primary School, Crawley

The Magic Box
(Based on 'Magic Box' by Kit Wright)

I will put in the box . . .
The dream of a bear,
The scent of a red, red rose
And the first tear of a baby.

I will put in the box . . .
The footsteps of my strong father,
The love of God
And the last smile of my loving mum.

My box is fashioned from diamonds and crystals and gems,
With rainbows on the lid and God's blood in the corners.
Its hinges are lungs, the lungs of a sparkly, silver fish.

Connor Grant (8)
Milton Mount Primary School, Crawley

Pets

Dogs are very fun
They are always playing games,
They run all day long.

Cats play with a ball
And always have a long nap,
Most cats are quite fat.

Hamsters play at night
They sleep during the daytime
And run on a wheel.

Ferrets play all day
And sleep at night-time like us,
Because ferrets rule.

Guinea pigs are fast
They zoom energetically,
They are very kind.

Kieran Armstrong (11)
Milton Mount Primary School, Crawley

The Magic Box
(Based on 'Magic Box' by Kit Wright)

I will put in the box . . .
The kindness from my mum,
The tip of a colour out of the rainbow
And the last smile from my dad.

I will put in the box . . .
The coldness of a white-snow polar bear,
The tip of the bluest bluebell
And the first sound of a baby.

My box is fashioned from rubies, kings and gems,
With a moon on the lid and wishes in the corners,
Its hinges are the jaws of a bright blue whale.

Amy Johnson (7)
Milton Mount Primary School, Crawley

The Cat

Tree climber
Mouse catcher
Rain liker
Bath hater

Bird catcher
Fish eater
Milk drinker
Curtain ripper

Wall scraper
High jumper
Good cuddler
Book tearer
Homework eater.

Sam Briggs (9)
Milton Mount Primary School, Crawley

The Magic Box

(Based on 'Magic Box' by Kit Wright)

I will put in the box . . .
The play from a polar bear cub,
The freshness of a spring plant
And the first pain of a baby.

I will put in the box . . .
The snuffle of a hedgehog,
The coldness of Jack Frost
And the light of the moon.

My box is fashioned from ambers, quartz and emeralds,
With moonflowers on the lid and love in the corners,
Its hinges are the beak of a red spotted woodpecker.

Emily Hawkins (7)
Milton Mount Primary School, Crawley

The Magic Box
(Based on 'Magic Box' by Kit Wright)

I will put in the box . . .
The prance of a polar bear,
The sharpness of a thorn
And the screams of a newborn baby.

I will put in the box . . .
The magic of a wizard,
A blood killing dinosaur
The love of a mother lioness.

My box is fashioned from lava and rainbows and fire,
With blackness on the lid and God's breath in the corner.

Gurben Sra (7)
Milton Mount Primary School, Crawley

The Magic Box
(Based on 'Magic Box' by Kit Wright)

I will put in the box . . .
The first growl of a snow-white bear,
The first swish of a green plant
And the first heart of a smile from a baby.

I will put in the box . . .
The colours of a rainbow,
The magic of a fairy
And a spark of a firework.

My box is fashioned from sapphire, emerald and ruby,
With moons on the lid and wishes in the corners,
Its hinges are a parrot's bright yellow beak.

Beth Hicks (7)
Milton Mount Primary School, Crawley

Man United

Man United are the best
We always finish above the rest.
Our manager's cool,
While Arsene Wenger will just simply drool.
We leave people to eat our dust
While Chelsea are left to completely rust.
We are cool, we are cool,
Much cooler than Hartlepool.
When we play them it's just boo, boo, boo,
We know how to kick a ball.
Newcastle only know how to play pool.
Man United aren't still in school
Learning how to kick a ball.
While Liverpool are still in school
Forgetting how to kick a ball.
So support Man U who are the best
Because we're better than all the rest.

Christopher Beaton (10)
Milton Mount Primary School, Crawley

The Magic Box
(Based on 'Magic Box' by Kit Wright)

I will put in the box . . .
The step of a snow-white polar bear,
The scent of a green plant
And the first look of a baby.

I will put in the box . . .
The footprints of my strong father,
The love of God
And the last smile of my loving mum.

My box is fashioned from sapphire and coal and crystals,
With a breeze from God on the lid and silk in the corners,
Its hinges are the tail of a scattering mouse.

Joel Lovelock (8)
Milton Mount Primary School, Crawley

Monday Morning

Monday morning
Is so boring
I am sighing
I am yawning

Sally's skipping
Karl's kicking
Warren's wailing
Julie's jumping

Monday morning
Is so boring
I am whining
I am weeping

Liam's leaping
Robyn's running
Peter's punching

Oh not another Monday morning.

Hayleigh Frith (10)
Milton Mount Primary School, Crawley

The Magic Box
(Based on 'Magic Box' by Kit Wright)

I will put in the box . . .
The dream of a growling bear,
The twinkle of a snow-white flower
And the first tooth of a baby.

I will put in the box . . .
A dream of a new life,
The love of my family
And the cry of a baby.

My box is fashioned from rubies and rings and gems,
With a moon on the lid and wishes in the corner,
Its hinges are the jaws of a bright blue whale.

Suzie Galvin (8)
Milton Mount Primary School, Crawley

Ginger

Ginger was a friend,
I thought he drove me round the bend,
Of course I was going to regret this,
I didn't really want this,
I didn't want him gone,
Erased from my life for evermore,
Ginger was a treasure box to me,
Inside of him were all my secrets revealed,
Now that he is gone,
He's in a better place,
At the age of 6,
You'd be surprised,
How much life pulled inside of him,
For evermore in my heart,
That's where he will stay,
'Cause when he died he tore part of me away,
The space will never be fulfilled,
No matter how hard I try,
My little rabbit Ginger,
Was not prepared to die!

Georgia Welch (11)
Milton Mount Primary School, Crawley

Sun

Life creator
Body sweater
Flame maker
Armour shiner
Enormous glower
Day sparkler
Fire lighter
Darkness hater
Inferno spreader.

Anand Lukhani (10)
Milton Mount Primary School, Crawley

My Idols

I have many idols
They are my favourite things
They're better than Holy Bibles
Or lots of golden rings.

> First of all is AJ
> Andy Johnson is his name
> He plays for Crystal Palace
> Football is his game.

Then Lucinda Green
Jumping high on horses
As a child she was keen
To jump high on those horses.

> After, Mrs Westlake
> My cool drama teacher
> She can be a snowflake
> Or a crying woman weeper.

I mentioned all my idols
But best is yet to come
Want to guess my idol?
Yes, of course, *my mum!*

Rae Degnan (11)
Milton Mount Primary School, Crawley

Night-Time

The sky is jet-black.
Most animals have to sleep
But jaguars are running in the shadows
And howler monkeys call to their mates.
It echoes through the rainforest.

Chloe Homewood (8)
Milton Mount Primary School, Crawley

My Friends

A for Andy who likes sugar and candy
B for Brian who has a pet lion
C for Clare who likes to stare
D for Daniel who has a cocker spaniel
E for Ellis who listens to Kellis
F for Freddie who has a teddy
G for Grace who fiddles with her lace
H for Harry who's real name's Barry
I for Ian who isn't European
J for James who likes to play games
K for Kate who doesn't have a mate
L for Lenny who found a penny
M for Mick who is thick
N for Niall who ran a mile
O for Ollie who has a parrot called Polly
P for Polly who has an owner called Ollie
Q for Quallien who is an alien
R for Ryan who is scared of a lion
S for Sam who likes Spider-Man
T for Tab who drives a cab
U for Una who gets there sooner
V for Vince who likes Polo mints
W for Will who watches 'The Bill'
X for Xabi who dresses shabby
Y for Yope who likes to climb ropes
Z for Zoe who lives where it's snowy.

Robin Laney (10)
Milton Mount Primary School, Crawley

Listen

Listen to the sounds.
Ants chopping the undergrowth.
Howler monkeys roaring loudly.
Butterflies fluttering among the exotic flowers.
Frogs croaking noisily and jumping in the cool water.

Hollie Lloyd (8)
Milton Mount Primary School, Crawley

Environment

E nvironment is where we live,
N ever will the moon disappear,
V eering here and everywhere,
I f we keep our environment tidy we will be healthy,
R eading, writing, learning, playing,
O n Earth we live
N ever will the Earth be in darkness,
M oonlight covering the Earth in a silvery blanket,
E veryone laughing and playing,
N othing worth missing,
T otal darkness at night except the moon and shimmering stars.

Earth is where we live,
It's a bright, colourful world.

Oceans and streams flow along,
Take a swim in the sea,
Or have a paddle in a pool.

Earth is where we live,
It's a bright, colourful world.

Emma Harding (10)
Milton Mount Primary School, Crawley

A Glimpse In A Rainforest

Listen to the forest sounds.
Noisy toucans squawking loudly in the canopy.
Marching leaf-cutter ants vibrate the forest floor.
Slithering anacondas coil round their prey and squeeze.
Jet-black panthers pounce with deadly skill.

Alana Cameron (8)
Milton Mount Primary School, Crawley

In The Land Of Make-Believe

Once in my dream, I went somewhere
The land of make-believe
There's lots to see like TVs with hair
In the land of make believe.

There's a chair that runs away
And trees the colour red
Buildings made out of hay
And people fly on a bed.

The clouds are like a marshmallow
A pig that sings a song
A lamp post that looks like a fellow
And a book that's always wrong.

There's a mouse that chases dogs
Stories that never end
A bunch of talking frogs
And you're bound to make a friend.

I loved my time there
They even gave me a hen
I won't even tell a single hair
But I know I'll return again!

James Seymour (10)
Milton Mount Primary School, Crawley

The Winter Poem

In the cold air people get bright red lips and icy.
The cars are icy, wet and the ice is cold and strong.
The pavement and roads are slippery - you have deep, deep snow,
The windows are covered in frost, benches full of snow.
When you go out you get covered in sparkling, wet and icy snow.
It is good outside and fun in the snow,
But it is also cold outside in the snow.
It is good fun in the snow.

Emily Wright (10)
Milton Mount Primary School, Crawley

What They Say On Pancake Day

My brother would say . . .
It smells yummy,
It tastes scrummy,
What could it be?
It's a pancake!

My sister would say . . .
Sugar and lemon,
Syrup is sellin',
What could it be?
It's a pancake!

I would say . . .
It's Pancake Day soon,
They're as big as the moon,
What could it be?
It's a pancake!

We all say . . .
Now that the day is almost done,
We're all stuffed and sad,
But look on the bright side,
There's always next year,
So let's all go mad!

Charlotte Milham (10)
Milton Mount Primary School, Crawley

A Glimpse In A Rainforest

Slimy frogs paddle in swampy water.
Squawking toucans fly from tree to tree.
Horrid anacondas squeeze their prey to death.
The chameleon changes colour to protect itself.
The acrobatic howler monkeys make a deafening howl.

Joe Gardiner (9)
Milton Mount Primary School, Crawley

I Would Like To . . .

I would like to taste the scream of football fans.
I would like to taste the sorrow of the rain
And the happiness of the breeze.
I would like to hear a plant grow.
I would like to hear a grape's opinion of being eaten.
I would like to paint the sting of a scorpion.
I would like to paint the smell of oranges.
I would like to touch the smell of lemons.
I would like to touch the smell of a tiger's breath.
I would like to eat the fluffiness of a cloud.

I would like to climb Mount Everest.
I would like to eat snow and ice in winter.
I would like to eat chocolate all day.
I would like to travel the world.
I would like to go to Barbados.
I would like to own my own sweet shop.
I would like to run in the Olympic Games.
I would like to help poor people.

Holly Talbut-Smith (8)
Milton Mount Primary School, Crawley

Snow Days

Cold, cold day,
With deep, white snow,
Frost on your car,
With icy, white snow,
Playground fields, hard as rock,
With slippy, white snow,
Tree branches bent,
With heavy white,
Filled with water,
From melting white,
Sharp, fast breeze
Brings more white snow.

Pranay Patel (9)
Milton Mount Primary School, Crawley

Magic Land

One day I swam with a dolphin,
Then I jumped in glee,
I tossed and turned and rolled around
And even smelled the sea.

The next minute I was riding a chestnut,
Over the Milky Way
And stopped to say hello
To a TV waiting to pay.

In my bed awake,
Realising it was a dream,
The dolphin and the horse
And wondering what the next would be,
Fell asleep in mystery,
In a land of glore,
Waiting for the next adventure,
To leap out the door.

Chloe Casey (11)
Milton Mount Primary School, Crawley

The English Fellow

Red,
Blue,
Green,
Yellow,
Describe an English fellow.

Every night by the fire
He sits and thinks in desire.

He wears an Australian hat
And sits and prays on a textured mat.

He speaks a different language,
He's the English fellow.

Georgie Baker (9)
Milton Mount Primary School, Crawley

A Glimpse Inside A Rainforest

Squawking, screeching toucans
Fight over brilliant coloured fruits.
Speckled tree frogs
Inflate throats and make loud croaks.
Acrobatic howler monkeys
Make a blood-curdling scream.
Clever camouflaged chameleon's prey
Sticks like glue to uncurled tongues.
The eagle swoops
And pierces its prey with sharp talons.

Joshua Weaver (9)
Milton Mount Primary School, Crawley

Monday Mornings

Jumpers flying,
Babies crying,
Sausages frying.

Shoes missing,
Cats hissing,
Dogs are barking back.

10 more minutes,
Where's my bag?
Where's my lunch box?
My brother just called me an old hag!

All I did,
Was fill his socks,
With my dad's . . .
Shaving cream!

Georgina Allen (11)
Milton Mount Primary School, Crawley

How To Avoid Kissing Your Parents In Public!

Say that your friends will be watching,
Say that they're near and can see,
Pretend to sneeze,
Say look at your keys,
Pretend to itch and have fleas.

Say that your lips are so sore,
Say that your cheek feels red roar.
Run away screaming,
Your smiley face beaming,
Teeth that are sparkly and gleaming.

Charlotte Croft (11)
Milton Mount Primary School, Crawley

Cat Kennings

Post scratcher
Mouse catcher
Long snoozer
Toy loser
Litter chaser
Garden racer
Hates water
Fish slaughterer
Fluffy cuddles
Splashing puddles
Loves milk
Furry silk
Loud screecher
Warm creature.

Emma Costello (9)
Milton Mount Primary School, Crawley

My Fave Things

I have many fabulous faves
And many great dreams to fulfil,
I'll tell you my top five faves,
At number six would be to chill,
But anyway here goes my tops.

       At number five there is lots of money,
       It's great and fun to spend all day,
       I want so much money, it's funny,
       Go and find nice stuff and then pay,
       That's what I chose as number five.

At number four there's fab footie,
I love to spend all day and play,
It's much better than dodgeball,
'It's fabulous!' that's what I say,
So that is a good number four.

       Number three is top lions, Chelsea!
       They are fab and are at the top,
       I think about them in the sea,
       I'll always choose them over pop,
       So there, you now have my number three.

At number two there's Frank Lampard,
He is really sexy and fit,
I want him in my birthday card,
He looks very nice in his kit
And now you have my second fave thing.

       You're waiting for my number one,
       After you heard all the others,
       I enjoy having them it's fun,
       They are so great, they need no cover,
       My number one is my friends and family!

Emma Clark (10)
Milton Mount Primary School, Crawley

Winter Poem

Winter sounds like a cold
Breezy morning with someone
With a hot mug of tea.

Winter feels fun and boring
Unlike a hot summer's day.

Winter tastes like
Cold and snowy air.

Winter smells like ice melting
So it smells watery.

Winter looks like a cold
And snowy day with ice.

Winter reminds me
Of summer but cold.

Bhavik Lakhani (9)
Milton Mount Primary School, Crawley

Green Day

Green Day are the best,
Better than all the rest!
Mike always wears a vest,
But gets the girls impressed!

As Billy leads the show
His fans give him a big, 'Wow!'

Tre Cool is the drummer
And no, he's not a plumber!
Once he got an electric wire
And set his drums on fire!

Stephen Gilchrist (10)
Milton Mount Primary School, Crawley

My Holidays Away From Home

My holidays are always great,
Because I meet cool mates,
When I'm swimming in the pool
And if not a fool.

And I am having a laugh,
Not at school doing a task
And not in the cold drinking from a flask.

I'm lying on the beach getting a tan,
Or if not, I'm lying asleep with a cool fan.

My holidays away from home!

Matthew Keating (10)
Milton Mount Primary School, Crawley

Dark In The Forest

At night in the jungle
Some hunters become the hunted.
Anacondas squeeze their prey
Explorers sleep peacefully.
Herbivorous monkeys get caught
By an eagle and its brilliant eyesight!

Henry Yeomans (9)
Milton Mount Primary School, Crawley

A Glimpse Into A Rainforest

Leaves rustling in the canopy.
Slimy snakes wrapping themselves round slippery branches.
Shiny raindrops falling from the sky.
Butterflies fluttering round and round.
Monkeys swinging high in the canopy.

Jodie Cashman (9)
Milton Mount Primary School, Crawley

Mystery Footballer

S uperlative
O verwhelming
L oads of skill, England team player

C ool
A gile
M y hero
P rofessional
B rilliant
E xcellent, he's great
L oaded
L et's have a guess.

Yes, it's . . .
Sol Campbell!

Peter Warnock (10)
Milton Mount Primary School, Crawley

Rainforest Animals

Tropical thunderstorms roaring through the night.
Capybaras gracefully springing into action.
Toucans motionlessly gliding through the air.
Eagles unmercifully grip their prey with their talons.
Minute, leaf-cutter ants hunting for their prey.
Monkeys acrobatically swinging from canopy to canopy.

Blaise Salle (8)
Milton Mount Primary School, Crawley

Winter

White snow, freezing weather
My friends hugging each other
My feet on the playground freezing
The boys skidding with each other.

Georgia Simmonds (9)
Milton Mount Primary School, Crawley

By The Spooky Swamp

Croaking frogs squelch in the mud,
Fish jump up into the air
Then dive back into the shimmering water,
Chameleons flick out their tongues
And catch their prey,
Alligators snap their jaws in the murky water.

Haleigh Lembergs (8)
Milton Mount Primary School, Crawley

Winter's Wet

Winter's cold
Winter's wet
It feels like a frozen ice cube
Rain's on my window
Rain's everywhere
The puddles are like small swimming pools
Tomorrow will be sunny, not cold and muddy
But I still like winter
Even though it's windy and wet.

Nicole Laker (9)
Milton Mount Primary School, Crawley

Harriet

H arriet is mad,
A little bit sweet,
R ascal they say,
R attles about all day,
I think she's mad,
E ven though she
T alks all day.

Hannah Paton (10)
Milton Mount Primary School, Crawley

A Winter's Poem

Winter sounds like a snowflake going past my ear.
Winter smells like a cold, bitter day ahead of me.
Winter looks like an iceberg coming towards me at full speed.
Winter feels like a cold and bitter day.
Clothes wrapped around me, that will not let go of me
Until I get in a warm, loving home with all of my family.
Winter tastes like a frostbite on my tongue
And will not get off my tongue until I eat my lovely roast dinner.

Emma Osborne (10)
Milton Mount Primary School, Crawley

Winter Wonderland

Winter feels like an avalanche sucking you under.
Winter sounds like the Titanic clashing an iceberg.
Winter smells like the fire burning a marshmallow.
Winter tastes like snow melting on your tongue.
Winter looks like the freezing French Alps.
Winter reminds me of Snow White but no dwarfs.

Sophie Norris (9)
Milton Mount Primary School, Crawley

Snow Tanka

The snow is freezing
Snowflakes are falling off trees
People watch them fall
A white blanket on the ground
I wish snow fell all the time.

Karenjit Padda (10)
Milton Mount Primary School, Crawley

My Idol

A rsene Wenger is the best
R eyes has been put on rest
S enderos is on his own
E ven now he plays alone
N o matter what they say
A rsenal are on their way
L eaders Chelsea aren't going to win
   because Arsenal are going in.

R ay Parlor has left the team
O wen has had a dream
C ygan is so class
K icking the ball into glass.

Rhys Freeman (10)
Milton Mount Primary School, Crawley

Usher

Usher is so great
He is always number one
Everyone shouts, 'Well done!'
They all want to be his boo
When he says his Confessions Part 2.

He wears loadsa solid bling
When he dances it goes ching ching
All the girls scream
As though it may seem
He will always be the best.

He is fab at everything
Singing, dancing and raps
He is an R&B star
Who gets very far
With the talent he has he is the king!

Kimberley Logan (11)
Milton Mount Primary School, Crawley

Friends

Friends are the key of life,
They help you through good and bad,
But when they leave it's the worst thing.

You feel empty inside,
Like your heart has been taken out and stabbed 1000 times,
It's like no pain ever before.

But when you get that letter,
Your heart fills with joy.
You read it and read it again,
You feel like the world is once more on your side.

You find whatever piece of paper and a pen,
You write and write,
Your hand can't stop writing.

You're finished, but you can't find an envelope,
You call for Mum,
She tells you where they are,
You grab one and run to the postbox.

Now all your life you read, you write,
You read, you write,
You read, you write.

Katie Steed (11)
Milton Mount Primary School, Crawley

Blossom

A lovely spring evening under the blossoming tree
With the bright moon coming down on me.
The beautiful red roses with all their pride and joy
While I sit on a bench with my boy.

Gabrielle Martin (8)
Ocklynge County Junior School, Eastbourne

Friendship

Friends are good
Friends always should
Support each other
Like sisters and brothers.

Friends stick together
Through thick and thin
Whether they lose
Or whether they win.

Friends sometimes fight
But will always mend
Because friends will be friends
Right to the end.

Kelly Snow (9)
Ocklynge County Junior School, Eastbourne

Ocklynge School

Ocklynge School
It's time to get in the swimming pool.
If you want to mix in
You will have to do the gym.
So get out of bed and use your head.
Open your book and have a look.
You can learn at every turn.
Class is fun just like a bun.
Ocklynge School
Ocklynge School
It's so cool!

Oska Eames (7)
Ocklynge County Junior School, Eastbourne

Spiders

Spiders, spiders everywhere.
In my attic, in my kitchen.
Under my bed, in my toilet.
Big spiders, small spiders,
Massive spiders, just spiders,
Just everywhere.
Cobwebs everywhere,
Cobwebs on the door handles,
Cobwebs on the ceiling.
Thin cobwebs, thick cobwebs,
Silky cobwebs, cobwebs everywhere.
I wish my mum used the duster
But, she likes the little things everywhere.

Paul Blackwell (8)
Ocklynge County Junior School, Eastbourne

Sunflowers

Yellow sunflowers just like the sun,
Now I have just begun.
Leave the sun shining on my sunflower,
Let the rain pour down,
Then my sunflower will have a shower.
The wind makes a breeze,
It sways in the night,
Then it turns light.
Leave the rain showering down,
See it from your window,
See it from the trees,
See it blowing in the breeze.

Adelaide Morgan (7)
Ocklynge County Junior School, Eastbourne

My Dog Tigger

'Write about your brothers and sisters,' said the nursery teacher.
I didn't have any brothers or sisters
So I wrote about 'My Dog Tigger'.

Tigger, she eats chocolates out of advent calendars
And pulls up orange lino.
Pulls Mummy over when we are taking her out for walks.
Rips the sleeve of Daddy's coat.
Always whines when we eat our food.
Takes towels off radiators and uses them for beds
And our spaniel Tigger, scratches the paint from kitchen doors.

But when she looks at me
With those big, round eyes of hers,
I can't help but know
That she is the most wonderful dog in the *world*.

She plays hide-and-seek with me, Mummy and Daddy,
Runs up to me when I come home from school.
When I stay away for the night, she wakes up Mummy and Daddy
Because she loves me and wants to know where I am.
She guards the house
And barks when anyone comes nearby.
She sits next to me when I am ill
And comforts me when I cry.

So when she looks at me
With those big, round eyes of hers,
I can't help but know
That she is the most wonderful dog in the *world*.

Meggie Dennis (8)
Ocklynge County Junior School, Eastbourne

A Strange Creature

I have never seen a creature just like this before,
He came to my house and knocked at my door.
He was big, round and hairy and smelt of glue,
But he was very polite and said, 'How do you do.'
The smell was so strong I thought he'd need a shower,
Then he smiled so sweetly and gave me a flower.
He said, 'I love you, I love you and no other.'
What could I say? Oh dear, oh bother.
There was a strange silence and neither of us spoke,
I found myself yawning and stretching and then I awoke!
It was just a dream.

Antonia Fitzjohn (8)
Ocklynge County Junior School, Eastbourne

3D Children

Hannah Nunn had a mum that liked to have a bit of fun.
Everywhere would Hannah run and Mrs Nunn would also run.
Andrew Bruce had a moose who managed to get loose.
But Andrew's goose chased the moose that was on the loose.
Benicia Hall was very tall but James Hall was very small.
Benicia Hall liked playing with her ball.
But James Hall liked to play in the pool.

Sarah Reading (7)
Ocklynge County Junior School, Eastbourne

Fruit Pastlesaur

Fruit pastlesaur . . .
Is whiter than snow
Is faster than a tornado
Is sweeter than candyfloss
Is bigger than the Great Wall of China
Is more colourful than fruit
Is prettier than the rainbow.

Pascale Smith (8)
Ocklynge County Junior School, Eastbourne

Love

Love smells like roses
Love is peaceful in my heart
Love tastes spicy in my mouth
Love feels like smooth snow
Love smells like roses
Love is happy and feels like family together
Love is for your heart
Love is playing football with my friends
Love is riding Widgit
Love is peace for my mum and dad
Love smells like roses.

Sophie Pengilly (10)
Patcham House (Day Special) School, Brighton

Fear

Fear smells like stinky, lumpy, rotten fish.
Fear worries my heart and makes me trembly.
Fear tastes like a dry mouth and shivery lips.
Fear stops me being happy.
Fear stops me being excited.
Fear makes me unkind.
Fear helps me stay away from big spiders.

Harrison Austen-Evans (9)
Patcham House (Day Special) School, Brighton

Hate

Hate is ill and white
Hate stops your game
Hate tastes like nasty fish
Hate looks like an enormous aeroplane
Hate reminds me of being bored and lonely.

Paris Carroll (7)
Patcham House (Day Special) School, Brighton

Love And Hate

Love smells like a dark red rose that's been picked in the morning.
Love tastes like curry plants that have just bloomed.
Love sounds like flowers blowing in the wind.
Love looks like a baby being cuddled by his parents.
Love reminds you of a good time you had in the past.
Love stops you breaking someone's heart.

Hate tastes like a foul chunk of cheese that's gone stale.
Hate smells like a pocketful of mothballs
                        that have been left there for years.
Hate sounds like a bulldozer crashing down a building.
Hate looks like sisters and brothers hitting one another.
Hate reminds you of a bad time in the past.
Hate stops you from seeing someone as a friend again.

Jack Wright (11)
Patcham House (Day Special) School, Brighton

Fear And Love

Fear is being alone and sad.
Love is playing 'fetch' with my dog.

Fear is having a bad dream and crying to find my dad.
Love is when I'm with my family and my friends.
Fear smells like hot, sweaty air.
Love smells like my mum and dad's hugs.

Fear is the colour of an evil pitch-black field.
Fear reminds me of a bad dream that never ends.
Love reminds me of people in my street.
Love is the colour of soft red roses.

George Bolger (8)
Patcham House (Day Special) School, Brighton

Anger

Anger tastes like a dry hairball and dust in my mouth.
Anger is the colour of a dark black in the air.
Anger smells like a rotten piece of green hardened cat food.
Anger stops me having fun and laughter.
Anger reminds me of misunderstandings in my life.
Anger looks like a lot of lava coming down the hill.
Anger is helped by a separate room in a silent place
                            where no noise can reach me.

Nathan Lovegrove (11)
Patcham House (Day Special) School, Brighton

Love

Love reminds me of red salty crisps.
Love feels like strong muscles.
Love feels good.
Love smells like chocolate chip cookies.
Love tastes like soft and squidgy crisps.
Love looks like soft yellow flowers.
Love sounds like tapping feet.

Jamie Bourne (10)
Patcham House (Day Special) School, Brighton

What Is Red?

What is red?
Roses and love.
What is blue?
The sea and a teardrop.
What is orange?
The sun and excitement.
What is black?
Midnight and sorrow.

Emily Waters (9)
Rose Green Junior School, Bognor Regis

What Is . . . ?

What is wobbly?
A little girl's tooth.

What is gigantic?
A skyscraper's roof.

What is graceful?
A bird overhead.

What is snuggly?
Cuddling in my bed.

What is energetic?
My dog running on the beach.

What is frustrating?
My football out of reach!

What is upsetting?
My best friend feeling ill.

What is dangerous?
My dad with a drill!

What is smooth?
A stone washed by the sea.

What is amazing?
Someone like me!

Leah Minett (8)
Rose Green Junior School, Bognor Regis

Why?

Why is the sea as salty as a crisp?
Why is the moon round as a button?
Why are leaves green as grass?
Why do dogs bark and cats miaow?
Why do I wonder why?
Why do I start as a baby?
Why do we have to die?

Ellie Edwards (8)
Rose Green Junior School, Bognor Regis

Autumn Leaves

How do autumn leaves feel?

Brittle, fragile, light,
They crumble through your fingers,
Like a promise being broken.

How do autumn leaves sound?

Crickle, crackle, crunch,
In a gentle breeze they slowly sway,
Like waves on a calm day.

How are autumn leaves coloured?

Gold, yellow, red,
Hand-chosen, unique shades,
Painted just for this season.

How do autumn leaves fall?

Gently, sadly, inevitably,
Old, frail and damaged,
They give up their spirit.

Alice Bugeja (9)
Rose Green Junior School, Bognor Regis

Happiness And Sorrow

What is happiness?
Spending Christmas in a crowd.
What is sorrow?
The lonely number one.
What is happiness?
Playing rounders beneath the sun.
What is sorrow?
The world departed from fun.
What is happiness?
Me cuddling my dad and mum.

Joe Woods (11)
Rose Green Junior School, Bognor Regis

Rainbow Colours

What is red?
Red is the colour of my face on a hot summer's day.
What is yellow?
Yellow is the fire flickering in my lounge.
What is pink?
Pink is the colour of a newborn baby.
What is green?
Green is the grass getting mowed in spring.
What is orange?
Orange is the sun setting in the sky.
What is purple?
Purple is the velvet cloak upon the Queen's shoulders.
What is blue?
Blue is the colour of my brother's favourite football team.
What is a rainbow?
Rainbows are all of these colours.

Hayley Kent (10)
Rose Green Junior School, Bognor Regis

What Is Magical?

What is magical?
The magical cupboard.
What is the magical cupboard?
A place that is filled with joy.
What is joy?
The safety net beneath your fall.
What makes you fall?
A stone of sorrow at your feet.
What is sorrow?
A hole deep down inside.
How did that hole get there?
Through anger, hurt and loneliness.

Victoria Halsey (10)
Rose Green Junior School, Bognor Regis

My Questions

What is soft?
A sweet voice singing a song.

What is snuggly?
My bed.

What is strange?
A person dressed up in black.

What is interesting?
Reading in my head.

What is scary?
Knowing one day you'll die.

Chloe Archer (9)
Rose Green Junior School, Bognor Regis

What Is Hard?

What is hard?
Taking salt out of the sea,
Facing the truth,
Being stung by a bee.
What is easy?
Brushing your hair,
Painting a picture,
Not being fair.
What is sad?
When someone dies,
Being bullied,
A baby cries.
What is anger?
A new, broken toy,
Being told to do work,
Being without any joy.
What is excitement?
A party with friends,
Going on stage,
Days that don't end.

Laura Gibbs (9)
Rose Green Junior School, Bognor Regis

The Rainforest

Where do you find plants that never drop their leaves?
Where do animals do as they please?
Where do you find birds that are so bright?
Where do you find birds who have pillow fights?
Where does the beautiful ocelot live?
Where is the giant who has something to give?
Where do creatures with long tails hang?
Where is the animal called the orang-utan?
Where do all these creatures belong?
In the lush green land full of birdsong.

Heather Curtis (8)
Rose Green Junior School, Bognor Regis

Multicoloured

What is red?
Red is the colour of strawberries,
Red is anger swelling up inside me.
What is orange?
Orange is the beak of a crow,
Orange is the warm glow inside me when I'm happy.
What is yellow?
Yellow is the sun shining on our planet,
Yellow is the brightness inside me.
What is green?
Green is the grass in my garden,
Green is the jealousy inside me.
What is blue?
Blue is the colour of the sky,
Blue is the colour of my tears.
What is purple?
Purple is the colour of my room,
Purple is me when I'm in party mode.
What is multicoloured?
Multicoloured is excitement,
Multicoloured is my life!

Hannah Stride (9)
Rose Green Junior School, Bognor Regis

What's The Meaning Of All These?

Why don't fishes fly?
Why don't monkeys cry?
Why are we here on Earth?
Do we have a second birth?

Why are we at school?
Why have snooker when we have pool?
Why is the sun hot?
Why is ice not?

Why are the leaves on trees?
What is the purpose of disease?
Why is it money we always seize?
Tell me now please, what is the meaning of these?

Eleanor Jupp (10)
Rose Green Junior School, Bognor Regis

What Is?

What is curiosity?
Everything around you.
What is water?
A deep hole full of answers.
What is happiness?
Your heart getting lighter and lighter.
What is a family?
Warmth, friendship and love.
What is anger?
Fire burning, getting hotter and hotter.
What is this world?
Feelings stored in a box.
What is this poem?
Truth, life and from my soul!

Bethany Hirons (10)
Rose Green Junior School, Bognor Regis

The Colour Of Me

What is red?
Roses, rubies and my anger
When separated from my friends.

What is yellow?
Sun, sand and happiness,
When I make someone proud.

What is pink?
Glossy lipstick, the sunset and embarrassment
When I get a question wrong!

What is blue?
The sky, the ocean and my sadness
When days are too short and grey.

What is white?
The moon, the snow and my emptiness
When I'm in an unknown situation on my own.

Hayley Jewson (11)
Rose Green Junior School, Bognor Regis

Where Would I Find . . . ?

Where would I find a wobbly tummy?
Inside me when I come in for a test!
Where would I find a bit of red anger?
On my livid face when my friend betrays me.
Where would I find my mad imagination?
Inside my head when I'm writing my stories.
Where will I find a fun friendship?
In my heart and in yours.
How will I face horrid fear?
Courage, courage, that's all it really takes.

Kathryn Everington (9)
Rose Green Junior School, Bognor Regis

Emotions

What is special?
Moments that you will never forget.

What is freedom?
Freedom is speaking your mind
And feeling the wind blow through your hair.

What is a champion?
A champion wins with pride and passion
On the path to glory.

What is happiness?
Happiness brings joy and laughter
To each and every one.

What is sadness?
Sadness is losing somebody you love.

What is special?
Special is
Life!

Ollie Greenlees (10)
Rose Green Junior School, Bognor Regis

Why? Why? Why?

Why do stars glisten in the midnight sky
and follow you as you pass by?
Why do lions roar with pride
and make the startled creatures hide?

Why do people break the law,
kill, steal and go to war?
What are the words that are whispered in the trees,
the song of the birds, flowers and bees?

Why do roaring waves crash into the stones,
angry and fiery, and having a moan?
Why is love such an intense emotion
that makes all bad troubles drown in the ocean?

Why do darting cats prowl around at night,
stalking their prey and giving them a fright?
How did God make the Earth in seven days,
and is He to be believed, the Man that we praise?

Claudia Dickens (10)
Rose Green Junior School, Bognor Regis

Rainbow Colours

What is red?
Roses are red, standing beautifully in the garden.
What is green?
Grass is green, neat and peacefully swishing from side to side.
What is orange?
An orange, ripe and juicy.
What is pink?
Yummy marshmallows, sticky and warm.
What is blue?
The sky is blue, moving softly.
What is yellow?
The sun is yellow, beaming with light.
What is white?
The snow is white, children playing and building snowmen!
What is brown?
The floor is brown, creaking slowly.
What is black?
A panther sneaking up on its prey.
What is indigo?
The sunset is indigo, shining brightly.

Lottie Greenlees (7)
Rose Green Junior School, Bognor Regis

What Is Pretty?

What is pretty?
Friendship and stars.

What is evil?
Goblins and Mars.

What is sadness?
Your best friend, ill.

What is funny?
A clown on the mill.

What is shocking?
A bang and a bump.

What makes you hurt?
Your brother giving you a thump.

What is scary?
A vicious dog.

What is still?
A weak, brown log.

What is hot?
The sun shining bright.

What is screaming?
Me getting a fright.

What is brilliant?
You and *me!*

Brook Sharp (7)
Rose Green Junior School, Bognor Regis

What Is Safe?

What is safe?
Money in a bank, safely stacked.
What is dangerous?
The capital city in Iraq.
What is safe?
Being at home.
What is dangerous?
Being left out alone.
What is safe?
Jewels in a box under lock and key.
What is dangerous?
A wild, rough sea.
What is safe?
Being with friends.
What is dangerous?
When the world ends.

Chris Cox (11)
Rose Green Junior School, Bognor Regis

Feelings Rainbow

What is blue? Sea and sadness.
What is red? Fire and fear.
What is green? Snakes and shame.
What is pink? Jelly and joy.
What is purple? Silk and shock.
What is yellow? Sun and truth.
What is black? The dark and death.
A rainbow of my feelings.

India Ede (11)
Rose Green Junior School, Bognor Regis

What Is Life?

What is life?
A cycle of emotions, up and down.
Is love what one feels for another,
Or a deception that steals your heart away?
Is sad an upside down world full of chaos and destruction?
Is hate a leaping tiger, snatching your life from your hands?
Where does loneliness come from,
The Devil or an angel?
Where has happiness gone?
The bottom of the puddle, the river, the sea?
Why has laughter gone?
Have the clenching fists of darkness
Taken our will to live with joy?
What is life?
Does the answer lay in wait in a distant world,
In a crater full of thoughts and fear?

Oliver Bateman (10)
Rose Green Junior School, Bognor Regis

Questions

Why is the sky blue?
Who made me and you?

Why is the wind cold?
Why do we grow old?

How do lights glow?
Why are snails slow?

Can your mind bend?
When will time ever end?

Joseph Martin (8)
Rose Green Junior School, Bognor Regis

What Is Sorrow?

What is sorrow?
The waves of the sea.
What is friendship?
You and me.
What is truth?
Owning up.
What is special?
Mum's favourite cup.
What is freedom?
Running around.
What is excitement?
A lost thing being found.
What is noisy?
The wind through the trees.
What is pain?
Grazing my knees.
What is empty?
A lost boy's heart.
What is full?
A fresh new start.

Ellis Georgeou (9)
Rose Green Junior School, Bognor Regis

What Is . . . ?

What is happiness?
A baby's cheeky laugh!
What is sadness?
A deep hole in your heart.
What is anger?
A dark cloud swelling up inside.
What is jealousy?
A raging fire glinting in your eyes.
What is nervousness?
A weak and fragile body.
What is frustration?
The gritting of your teeth.
What is tiredness?
Eyes getting heavier.
What are poems?
Bringing people together.

Rosie Hemming (11)
Rose Green Junior School, Bognor Regis

Soldiers At War

W eapons shooting everywhere,
A soldier dying in pain.
R age about the Germans.

S adness of not knowing if my family's OK.
O ther people suffering.
L oving families being separated.
D eath tearing families apart.
I n the shelters, people scared.
E veryone running for shelter.
R anting soldiers going mad.

Charlotte Roberts (10)
St Mark's CE Primary School, Brighton

A Soldier In The War

Houses falling down,
People dying all around me,
Burning boats on fire in the sea,
People running from bombs.

Frightened of what might happen next,
Pain from all of the bombs,
Terrified of not knowing if your family is alive or dead,
Scared with all the dead people around me.

People shooting guns,
Babies crying all around me,
People screaming loudly,
Aeroplanes crashing into high walls and hotels.

The burning of fire as the houses are flamed,
The smell of people who have rotted away in the fire,
Putting on our masks as the gas starts to spread,
The sweet smell of success as they win the war.

Lacey Cole (10)
St Mark's CE Primary School, Brighton

A War Soldier

W hat can you see?
A bullet shooting at someone,
R ange of people running at me.

S oldiers fighting,
O n the boats, people dying,
L iving children scared to death,
D ead people no longer in pain.
I n shelters people are scared,
E veryone rushing around,
R anting soldiers going mad.

Charlotte Rolf (10)
St Mark's CE Primary School, Brighton

A Soldier In The War

All the brave soldiers injured,
People crying in their shelters,
People screaming with pain,
And many homes destroyed.

I can feel the sadness of broken families,
I can feel fear about where the bombs will drop next,
I can feel blood dripping onto my leg.

I hear the noisy planes,
I hear the all-clear siren,
I hear the bombs dropping,
I hear crying with pain.

I smell the damp of the dark shelter,
I smell the smoke of fire
And the great smell of *victory!*

Bethany Dahr (10)
St Mark's CE Primary School, Brighton

A Soldier At War

Burning boats on the sea,
People running like a bee,
People putting on their masks,
People doing all their tasks.

Sadness, not knowing if families are still alive,
Frightened, getting ready to dive,
Conscious, getting ready to shoot,
Feeling myself putting on my boots.

Bombs crashing all around me,
People screaming that I can see.
Bullets shooting all around me,
Sirens flashing, all in the war.

Zoe Fortune (9)
St Mark's CE Primary School, Brighton

A Soldier At War

What can you see?
Burning boats on the sea,
People running in agony,
Bomb shelters over there,
Gas spreading everywhere.

What can you feel?
I feel scared that I might die,
I worry that my family is not alive.
I want to go home,
I don't want to be alone.

What can you hear?
People screaming all around,
Bullets flying, no one to be found,
Sirens whirring in my ear,
I can feel nothing, except fear.

Emma Holdway (9)
St Mark's CE Primary School, Brighton

A Soldier In The War

Burning boats in the sea,
People running from bombs,
Blood all over all roads,
Mothers getting carried to First Aid.

Sadness, not knowing if the families are safe,
Frightened, not knowing what's to be next,
Worried about how many are going to die,
Annoyed with seeing all the pain.

Mothers and children screaming down the lane,
Screaming bombs from the planes,
Bullets shooting in the air,
Sirens going off everywhere.

Courtney Moffett (9)
St Mark's CE Primary School, Brighton

Bombs In The War

Can you see?
Everyone shaking because they are scared of the bombs,
People dying all around me,
Kids with gas masks on, scared because
Their family is not there for them.

What can you feel?
A damp room with damp seats,
And cold, no food or drink for us.
We all could be in here for two or three whole hours.

You can hear?
Aeroplanes crashing into tall hotels,
Bombs firing at houses,
People screaming all the time
And sirens whirring.

The smell is?
Of bombs and fire,
And damp seats where
They have to sit.

Lacie-May Snow (9)
St Mark's CE Primary School, Brighton

A Soldier In The War

What can I see?
I can see frightened children crying,
People dying all around me.
I can see houses going up in flames,
Bomb shelters being blown to pieces.

What can I hear?
The wailing sound of the air raid sirens.
Rat-a-tat-tat of machine guns,
Planes crashing to the ground.

Jessie-Ellen Rutson (10)
St Mark's CE Primary School, Brighton

A Soldier In The War

Burning boats on the shore,
People running in fours,
People finding their masks,
People running around trying to do their tasks.

Sadness, not knowing if people are alive.
Nervous people walking in their homes to look for life,
Frightened, what is coming next?
Scared that the war will never be over.

Bullets in the air,
Sirens blaring through the mist.
People calling to go down to the air raid shelter,
Bombs that come falling down.

Katherine Jolly (9)
St Mark's CE Primary School, Brighton

Soldiers At War

W hat can you see?
A bomb dropping on my town,
R ange of people shooting at me.

S ad, not knowing if my family's alive.
O val gun pointing at me.
L iving children scared to death.
D ead people no longer suffering.
I n shelters people are scared.
E veryone in a rush to get to a shelter.
R anting soldiers going mad.

Lily Mateer (9)
St Mark's CE Primary School, Brighton

The Snow Queen

Icy cold an awaiting for fright,
the Snow Queen only comes out at night.
Freezing cold and winter comes,
the icy snow has just begun.
The Snow Queen has a frozen heart,
her lovely Kay to soon depart.
If you felt her cold, then it would kill you.
If you saw her power, then it would thrill you.
Her long white hair and her soft white skin,
she has the power to beckon you in.
You see her kingdom, walk through the door,
that is it - you are hers for evermore.
Icy cold and waiting for fright,
the Snow Queen only comes out at night.

Charlotte Ashurst (10)
St Nicolas CE Junior School, Portslade

The Forbidden Room

I step into the forbidden room,
The door closes with a creak.
Suddenly the lights switch off.
Pitch-black and then an ear-piercing scream.
I reach for the door.
I see a white figure,
Then a wolf running past, knocking me over.
I see nothing.
A howl echoes in the darkness as the
Door swings open and smoke gushes out . . .
Bang!

Courtney Franois (9)
St Nicolas CE Junior School, Portslade

The Barn Owl's Meal

He perches in the darkness
waiting until the rodent awakes,
and he sees the slightest movement.
He waits . . . and waits . . . and waits . . .
until the rodent moves!
He gets his wings ready and
his feathered body lowers down.
His sharp talons are hanging
over the edge of the rotten tree.
He fixes his eyes in the direction
of where the small mammal is going to run.
He flies to the closest tree and
his short neck looks down at the ground.
Then the rodent starts to run and
suddenly stops under the tree that
the barn owl is sitting on.
The barn owl again lowers his feathered wings,
his tail lifts up and he swoooooops down
to the confused rodent.
The barn owl catches the rodent
using his sharp talons.
Then the proud barn owl sits back
on the rotten tree and has a
good time eating his rodent!
Hopefully next time he will catch a larger prey!

Rhiannon Breeze (9)
St Nicolas CE Junior School, Portslade

Dolphins

I like dolphins, they can swim.
They are very sleek and slim.
I just cannot swim like that,
And that is an important fact.

Underwater they can speak,
Making noises from their beak.
When they're scared or terrified,
They can talk and then they'll hide.

Sharks can catch them from their space,
Then dolphins don't have much grace.
They can hide and they can run,
They can surface to the sun.

I *love* dolphins, they are kind,
If I were one I wouldn't mind.
I can see the children play
With the dolphins as they lay.

Zara Butt (10)
St Nicolas CE Junior School, Portslade

Aliens

A liens are scary,
L ooking for people to eat,
I nvading loads of people,
E ating like a sheep.
N aughty all the time,
S ucking all their slime.

Ahh, I hate them!

Ashley Lidbetter (9)
St Nicolas CE Junior School, Portslade

I Don't Like Bed!

My mum says, 'Go to bed,'
So does my dad.
I really don't like going,
It makes me very mad.

'Kala keeps on talking,'
My little sister cries.
What do they expect me to do,
Lay down and close my eyes?

Sometimes I like to sing a song
By Natasha Bedingfield,
But it seems that everyone would like it more,
If I kept my mouth sealed.

And if I dare to leave my bed,
My mum and dad go really red.
'Kala, that's it, you are grounded.'
Do they know how mean they sounded?

I want to dance,
I want to prance,
I want to sing and shout.
I want to jump around the room
And wave my arms about.

I hate to go to sleep,
I hate to go to bed,
I think it is a waste of time,
I'd rather play instead.

Kala Gallacher (9)
St Nicolas CE Junior School, Portslade

Enchanted Forest

Over hills and countryside,
There's an enchanted forest
Where unicorns spread
Their glittery magic across the leafy floor.

Trees sway to the peaceful music
Of the hummingbirds' call,
Whilst they drop their tiny seeds
Where they wait for the fairy to
Spray their dust onto their tiny heads.

Fairies open their wings in the
Moonlit sky and flutter through the trees
Spreading their dust.

Unicorns splash by a stream,
Lighting up the water as they
Brush the water onto their shiny horns,
Making them glow in the darkness.

Leprechauns leap over their sparkly rainbows
To their shining gold at the end.
Dragons glide through the beautiful late sunset
Searching for their precious eggs.

This sounds like the perfect place,
But really there's no such thing.

Elizabeth Dillistone (10)
St Nicolas CE Junior School, Portslade

My Mum

My mum shimmers like a shining star
And drives around in a stunning, gorgeous car.
She's witty and wonderful, pretty as can be, just like me
If we were together now, how happy we'd be!

Rosie Nicholson (9)
St Nicolas CE Junior School, Portslade

Enchanted Wood

A wood hidden from sight, so peaceful,
Showered by the sun's bright light.
You would not hear a word or sound
Except the leaves crumpled on the ground.
A faint sound catches your ear,
You can hear a waterfall flowing near.
But an enchanted wood is never the same
Without a white unicorn with a silvery mane.
Look at the trees, they're a beautiful sight,
Swaying all day and swaying all night.
Out of the trees the birds will fly,
Up and up, straight into the sky.

Abigale Oakley (10)
St Nicolas CE Junior School, Portslade

Colours

What is yellow?
Yellow is the sunshine
Blazing with hotness.

What is blue?
Blue is the sea
Shimmering in the sun.

What is green?
Green is the grass
Being trampled on.

What is red?
Red is a ruby
Waiting to be sold.

What is pink?
Pink is a kiss
From a person to another.

Hayley Hodges (9)
St Nicolas CE Junior School, Portslade

Call Of The Horn

The horn has been blown ready for the fight
As the warlords ready to fight with their might.
Swordsmen defending with each shield,
Who might be forced to yield.

Horsemen move closer and much more near,
And just might cause fear!
The princess breaks out a small sob,
As the brave warriors face the rampaging mob.

Rain starts to drip, then fall,
As the archers ready to wipe them all!
The wizard shoots lightning at the opposing foes,
When a hobbit shoots an arrow and hits an enemy's toes!

Charge!
The combat begins . . .

Holly Knight (11)
St Nicolas CE Junior School, Portslade

My Favourite Things

I like the stars and
All things bright,
I hate the dark,
I love the light.
I like the sun,
To watch it rise up,
I hate the grass unless it's cut.
I like the flowers
Standing tall,
I love nature,
I love it all!

Elisa Belluscio (9)
St Nicolas CE Junior School, Portslade

Things That Disappear

Things that disappear,
that is my fear.
Once second they're there,
and next they're nowhere.
What is your fear?
Is it things that disappear?

Things that disappear,
that is my fear.
When I hear sounds
and no one is around,
that is my fear.

When something's there,
and then it's nowhere,
it sends a shiver down my back,
and that is a true fact.

Things that disappear,
that is still my fear.
It creeps me out,
but not when I'm out and about.
Things that disappear.

Christina Cushing (9)
St Nicolas CE Junior School, Portslade

Love

Broken heart,
Just when you think it's right, it's wrong.
Your heart feels as if it's breaking.
You feel a part of you, you have not seen yet.
Love has broken in half!

Toni-Louise Richardson (11)
St Nicolas CE Junior School, Portslade

Air Raid

Legs shaking,
   Limbs stiffening,
      Arms cramping,
         Feeling depressed.

Planes hovering,
   Bombs dropping,
      People crying,
         Feeling depressed.

Cold tunnels,
   Dark spaces,
      Candles flickering,
         Feeling depressed.

Shaking body,
   Spine shivering,
      Sickly tastes,
         Feeling depressed.

People fidgeting,
   Getting up,
      Stairs are there,
         Feeling relieved.

Daisy Roberts (10)
St Nicolas CE Junior School, Portslade

My Little Doggy

My little doggy
Is really cute,
He likes to eat
And he likes the heat.
All the time he smiles,
He always picks up the phone and dials.
At bedtime he gets into bed
And dreams about his day ahead!

Georgia McNealy (9)
St Nicolas CE Junior School, Portslade

What Are You Scared Of?

What are you scared of?
Are you scared of the dark,
Or maybe it's just the park?
What are you scared of?

It's clashing, it's bashing!
What could it be?
It's creaking, it's leaking,
What could it possibly be?

I can't see a thing,
I'm so scared - it's starting to sting.
Leave me alone, just go away!
Leave me, leave me, go, go away!

Look, the light's on!
Thank goodness it's gone.
Look, that's what it was,
It was only my *mum*!

Rebecca Canneaux (10)
St Nicolas CE Junior School, Portslade

What I Love In This World

I love the flowers scattered around,
I love a spring morning, I love the sound.
I love to play out with my friends,
I hate it when the fun all ends.
I love the sun all bright and yellow,
I love the corn in a meadow.
I love the grass all dark and green,
I love these things which I have seen.

Maisy Johnsen (9)
St Nicolas CE Junior School, Portslade

The Diary Of A Soldier

1916, April 5

We have been at war for a long time now,
I wish I was at home.
All I hear is bombs banging,
Banging in the air.
I have got used to being in the mud
But I still hate it.
I hate there being sadness all around,
But I am very sad myself.
I have hope for my friend
For he is at war right now.
I hear a siren and I see my friend,
But he has gone to a better place.
I am at home now, I am still sad for the people at war,
My heart goes to them all the time,
But in my sleep I think, *why, why is there war?*

Maisie Chandler (10)
St Nicolas CE Junior School, Portslade

Chocolates

C is for caramel,
H is for hazelnuts,
O is for orange chocolate chip,
C is for cream,
O is for oozing soft centres,
L is for chocolate lime,
A is for almond nuts,
T is for toffee,
E is for Easter eggs,
S is for strawberry filling.

Holly Molloy (11)
St Nicolas CE Junior School, Portslade

Haunted

First we walk into the house
And it's as big as ten elephants, yet as quiet as my mouse.

Now we're in the first room,
Where ghosts meet and zombies loom.

Walking through the murky corridors,
With dusty walls and creaky floorboards.

Shivering up a few spiral stairs
Where one big, ugly monster lairs.

It's chasing us, let's run away!
It was a bad idea to come and stay!

Phew, at last, we're outta this house.
Oh no! I forgot about my mouse!

Andrew Connacher (10)
St Nicolas CE Junior School, Portslade

Listen

Silence is when you hear things, listen:

A flower opening at sunrise,
The grass growing under the sun,
My fingernails growing in the night,
A grasshopper jumping through the grass,
A leaf falling on the grass in autumn,
The sun rising in the morning.

Fern Ridge (9)
St Nicolas CE Junior School, Portslade

The Haunted Room

Blood dripping,
Footsteps creeping,
Calling whispers,
Freezing cold.

                Getting closer,
                Feeling scared,
                Trees rustling,
                Freezing cold.

Owls hooting,
Ghosts hovering,
Bones snapping,
Feeling scared.

Laura Andrews (11)
St Nicolas CE Junior School, Portslade

Tsunami

I can hear the people screaming for their families,
I can hear the cries of the babies.
I can feel the sadness all around me.
I can feel the loss of my family.
I can see the people on the street with no homes.
I can see children on their own.
I can hear the tears trickling down their cheeks
Then dripping onto the ground.
I can feel the wind blowing against me.
I can see the young children crying.
I wish it never happened.

Robert Phillips (10)
St Nicolas CE Junior School, Portslade

What Is Blue?

Blue is the sky, ever so high.
Blue is the water, so clean and fresh.
Blue is a pillow, so soft and fluffy.
Blue is the ink squirting on paper.
Blue are the clouds, so tender and proud.
Blue is the Earth, so big and round.

Blue is the colour of its kind.
Blue is clay, so hard and solid.
Blue is the heavens opening up.
Blue is the angel of peace coming down.
Blue is the colour of ice freezing.
Blue is the colour of dolphins' skin.

Blue is the sky on an inky night.
Blue is the shiny glass of an eye.
Blue is the lord of the light.
Blue is the Chelsea flag flying high.
Blue is the sign of freedom waiting to be found.
Blue is the colour of strength, using all its might.

Blue is the colour of a pearl, hidden away in the sea.
Blue is the twinkle in people's eyes.
Blue is the sapphire hidden in the caves.
Blue is the colour of honesty in people's minds.
Blue is the colour of sadness in people's hearts.
Blue is the colour of a lightning strike.

Blue is the colour of violets in a field.
Blue is the sea with sun shining.
Blue is an inky liquid, all blobby and gooey.
Blue is the colour of coolness running through the air.
Blue is the colour of the Brighton and Hove Albion.
And most of all, blue is just blue!

Jack Trimm (11)
St Nicolas CE Junior School, Portslade

Wind, Sunshine, Rain And Snow

When the breeze starts and the wind blows,
The quiet things start to speak,
Some howling, some whistling, some sound strong
And some whisper.

Grass is swishing,
Treetops sighing,
Flags are swaying and are snapping to the sky,
Wires and poles are clinging and clanging.

The wind is whistling whilst the bells are singing.

Lizzie Walker (11)
St Nicolas CE Junior School, Portslade

The Day

Morning.
The outside air.
Get up and watch TV
Eating up bread and cereal.
Yummy!

Lunchtime.
Finish homework,
Start reading my new book,
Playing with my PS2 game.
Wicked!

Bedtime.
Brushing my teeth.
I switch off the light switch
Then I go into my warm bed.
Comfy!

Samuel Lawrence (11)
St Nicolas CE Junior School, Portslade

Parents' Evening

My mum got dressed in her best clothes,
My dad sat down and did nothing at all.
My brother put his skating jeans on,
And I was just plain old me.

We got in the car and set off . . .

My mum shouting at my brother,
My dad complaining because he didn't want to go,
My brother telling my mum what to do,
And I was just plain old me.

We waited outside the classroom, waiting for our turn . . .

My mum looking at her watch,
My dad complaining because he was so bored,
My brother doing his thing,
And I was just plain old me.

We went in and sat down . . .

My mum hoping it was going to be OK,
My dad shivering from the cold,
My brother acting cool,
And I was just plain old me.

We finished the meeting and got in the car . . .

My mum praising me,
My dad trying to talk to Mum,
My brother wanting to go home,
And I was just plain old me.

We got home and went inside . . .

My mum tired,
My dad relaxing,
My brother playing music,
And I went straight to bed.

Kayleigh Elliott (10)
St Nicolas CE Junior School, Portslade

Running

Running all around,
Running here and there,
Running everywhere,
Stop and start again.

Running through the park,
Running through the town,
Running through the gate,
Running past your mate,
Stop and start again.

Running over the hill,
Running past the windmill,
Running through the park,
Stop and start again.

Running through the woods,
Running past the school,
Running past the swimming pool,
Stop and start again.

Running to the end,
Quickly around the bend,
Running past the finish line,
In your best ever time.

Chloe Parks (9)
St Nicolas CE Junior School, Portslade

Red

Red is a clown's nose,
Red is a big bright rose,
Red is a juicy cherry,
Red is a small berry
Red is big, red is bright,
Red makes lots of light.

Reece Ezobi (8)
St Nicolas CE Junior School, Portslade

I Can Hear . . .

I can hear my hair growing,
I can hear a red-back spider spinning a web in Australia.
I can hear someone licking an ice cream.
I can hear an ice cream melting.
I can hear a koala eating eucalyptus leaves.
I can hear an alien walking on the moon.
I can hear the Earth orbiting the moon.
I can hear the bright orange sun rising in the sky.

Jake Lawman (9)
St Nicolas CE Junior School, Portslade

Brighton, In The Premiership!

The crowd are cheering Leon Knight,
To me this game is like a fight.
The Premiership is there for us,
So we'll jump onto our team bus.
We will sign Wayne Rooney to our team,
And then we'll sign Robbie Keane.

George Fenton (11)
St Nicolas CE Junior School, Portslade

Losing Lives In Palestine

Bang, bang, there go the guns,
Day in, day out, watching people dying.
Bombs exploding in the air.
Holding guns at innocent people,
Homes being destroyed,
Waiting for Israelis to make more sadness.
People laying covered in blood,
People's tears trickling down each cheek,
Waiting for it to *stop!*

Louis Elkhatib (9)
St Nicolas CE Junior School, Portslade

Listen

Silence is when you hear things, listen:

A dog sleeping in the cold air,
A fly's wing moving calmly,
The squeak of a pencil touching the paper,
The school of fish gliding in a pond,
A candle's light beaming in the darkness,
A blackbird being born,
And best of all I can hear,
A group of mice in France eating a small feast!

Abigail Moles (9)
St Nicolas CE Junior School, Portslade

A Soldier During WWI

I just want to go home,
I just want to be safe.
The fear of knowing I could be shot any minute,
The wet grass beneath my feet,
The sound of bombs above me,
Knowing I might not wake up tomorrow.
Dead bodies all around me.
Just let me go home,
I beg of you.

Jack Moss (9)
St Nicolas CE Junior School, Portslade

Listen . . .

Silence is when you hear things, listen.

The stars twinkling in the moonlight,
The spiders spinning webs in the trees,
The wind blowing softly across the ocean,
A ladybird blinking gently in the morning,
An ant crawling on the floor.

Shane Boyce (8)
St Nicolas CE Junior School, Portslade

Hallowe'en

It was dark and cold on that Hallowe'en night,
People dressed up, trying to give me a fright.
Knocking on the door, saying, 'Trick or treat?'
Looking for something sweet to eat.

Knock, knock, my mouth goes dry,
I try not to let myself cry.
I start to shake and then to shiver,
I used to be scared, but now I am not.

Nicole Garoghan (9)
St Nicolas CE Junior School, Portslade

Yellow

What is yellow?
Yellow is the pollen inside a flower.
Yellow is a highlighter jotting across your page.
Yellow is the sun sparkling in the daylight.
Yellow is a bee flapping its wings.
Yellow is a strip on the Jamaican flag.
Yellow is the sand swerving on the beach.
Yellow is a buttercup swerving on the grass.
Yellow is the tasty cheese on a pizza.
How could we live without yellow?

Taylor Shorter (9)
St Nicolas CE Junior School, Portslade

Listen

Silence is when you hear things, listen:

Silence is an ant scurrying through the earth.
Silence is a green shoot coming through the soft soil in spring.
Silence is a spider making its sparkly web.
Silence is a ladybird walking on the green grass.

Jack Copping (8)
St Nicolas CE Junior School, Portslade

The Playground

One child sitting alone, watching in the cold,
Two children, racing brave and bold.
Three children sharing secrets, softly whispering,
Four children playing hairdressers, with hairclips glistening.
Five children are playing a chasing game, running, shouting,
Six children are having an argument, bellowing, pouting.
Seven children are fussing, worrying over tests,
Eight children are shooing others away, saying they're pests.
Nine children are eating, swapping for other snacks.
Ten children are being spiteful, whispering behind other's backs.

There is a fight on the playground, pushing and shoving.
But it should not be like that, it should be caring and loving.

Sammy Carden (10)
St Nicolas CE Junior School, Portslade

Snow

Tumbling out of the sky,
Quietly whistling down the chimney,
The frost crawling up the window,
Whispering through the tiny cracks in the bricks,
Falling on the bare branches,
Then sleeping on the ground.

Lydia Bunn (11)
St Peter & St Paul CE Primary School, Bexhill-on-Sea

Anger

Anger is red-hot bubbling lava.
It smells like blazing fire burning as time goes.
The sound of thunder rolling around the sky
And crashing waves against rocks.
Anger - like a volcano erupting,
Flaming hot spices ready to burn.

Lauren Inglis (10)
St Peter & St Paul CE Primary School, Bexhill-on-Sea

Wonders Of Nature

Mushrooms, like a snail shell,
Twirling in a spiral.

Bark like a map
Telling animals where to go.

A field of crops,
Like tents all in rows.

Rhododendrons -
A display of exploding fireworks.

Snowy white trees
Like a pile of snow,
Red berries
Like Rudolph's nose!

What a wonderful world.

Max Pritchett-Page (11)
St Peter & St Paul CE Primary School, Bexhill-on-Sea

Snow

The dancing snowflakes
Flutter downwards
Sparkling diamonds of light.

Look out the window!
The snow has put a chilly blanket
On top of the world.

People wrap up warm,
It's a cold night tonight.
Let's build a snowman.

Rebecca Freshwater (10)
St Peter & St Paul CE Primary School, Bexhill-on-Sea

Happiness

Happiness is
Looking up at the sky
To see the sun shining down.

Happiness is
Playing with my friends,
Running round and round.

Happiness is
Watching my dogs splash about
In the sea.

Happiness is
Having jelly and ice cream
For tea.

Happiness is
My family.

Savanna Smith (10)
St Peter & St Paul CE Primary School, Bexhill-on-Sea

Beautiful Wonders

A mushroom as smooth as a snail's shell,
A dinosaur's body of rough bark,
Flowers exploding like fireworks in the gloomy sky,
Aloe vera soft and smooth, but yet so strong
Standing alert like blades of grass,
An orchid, purple and soft
Like a face full of joy and happiness.
A pansy smooth and juicy like a kiwi full of love,
The beautiful wonders of the patterns of nature.

David Ammoun (10)
St Peter & St Paul CE Primary School, Bexhill-on-Sea

Sea

Walking along the soft sand,
Chewing up the pebbles in its path,
Jumping and smacking
Its long smooth fingers
Along the shoreline,
Scaring people as it sweeps
Under their feet,
Then suddenly all calm,
Like a baby asleep.

Douglas Benge (11)
St Peter & St Paul CE Primary School, Bexhill-on-Sea

Fire

An angry man
Pushing and throwing
Volcanic bursts of deadly fire.
Angrily it waits for another victim,
Screaming,
It releases another deadly punch
Until slowly it drifts
Into a peaceful sleep.

Oliver Howard (10)
St Peter & St Paul CE Primary School, Bexhill-on-Sea

Fire

Swiftly smacking at dry, crisp wood,
Picking at twigs and kindling,
Flames twisting and turning,
Like cars in a busy road.
Silent but deadly it slowly
Grasps victims,
Dancing menacingly, but beautiful.

Tom Payne (10)
St Peter & St Paul CE Primary School, Bexhill-on-Sea

Wind

Whistling through yacht masts,
Shivering windowpanes,
Tickling door frames,
Chattering noisily,
Swirling in a storm,
Howling and yelling,
Suddenly dying down,
Sleeping peacefully.

Katherine Skeates (11)
St Peter & St Paul CE Primary School, Bexhill-on-Sea

Sea

Clicking for some music,
Tickling the shells,
It rises yawning and
Stretching its watery arms,
Crash!
Tormenting the pebbles,
Punching and flicking,
Before wandering up the shore.

Greg Anderson (11)
St Peter & St Paul CE Primary School, Bexhill-on-Sea

Wind

Walking gently,
A silent whisper,
Becoming louder,
Whistling ferociously,
Howls chasing and *screaming!*
Arms grabbing at tree branches,
Stamping and lashing out
At passers-by.

Kallista Owen (11)
St Peter & St Paul CE Primary School, Bexhill-on-Sea

Divine (Fairtrade) Chocolate

Divine, divine, it's that chocolate,
But now it's mine.
Chocolate, chocolate, I'm glad you're mine,
You taste like a feast on my tongue.
As soft as silk and so lusciously smooth, yet so creamy,
Solid to liquid as you melt in my mouth.
Divine, divine is your pleasure,
The chocolate you eat, such a treasure.
So delicious I can't wait until next time!

Beverley Eatten (10)
St Peter & St Paul CE Primary School, Bexhill-on-Sea

Fire

Breathing in its house,
Jumping up and down,
Spitting and swaying,
Burning until age shrivels each flame,
New life is born,
Walking stems of orange and red,
Whine and whistle,
Until its fever engulfs the room.

Sophie McGinty (10)
St Peter & St Paul CE Primary School, Bexhill-on-Sea

Sea

Creeping to the shore,
Then suddenly lashing its fierce hand,
Spitting out white foam,
Prancing back,
Ready for its next strike.

Ashley Iddenden (10)
St Peter & St Paul CE Primary School, Bexhill-on-Sea

School At Night!

The silent midnight moon
Illuminates the moans.
The SAT paper sits,
Like someone lying in bed -
Waiting for the alarm to ring.
Screaming loudly,
The computer sounds
Like children having fun in the park.
Suddenly, hovering down the corridor,
The light breathes silently,
Bringing a feeling of warmth and safety,
(As a baby with his teddy bear).

Samuel Ball (11)
St Peter & St Paul CE Primary School, Bexhill-on-Sea

Divine (Fairtrade) Chocolate

Divine, divine, creamy, it's mine.
Slowly opening the soft chocolate
Breaking my first little bit to taste.
Melting on my tongue
Making my taste buds explode with joy.
Thanks to God
I've tried chocolate for the very first time.

Ian Coshall (10)
St Peter & St Paul CE Primary School, Bexhill-on-Sea

Snow

The cold-feeling snow tumbles down
As the wind whistles round the corner,
And children play, making things in the snow
Having fun all day long.
Adults gaze as children play,
Enjoying watching the cold snow fall.

Katie Robson (11)
St Peter & St Paul CE Primary School, Bexhill-on-Sea

Divine (Fairtrade) Chocolate

Divine chocolate,
There it was in my hand,
There it was in my mouth,
So smooth,
So lusciously soft,
I was hoping it would last forever.
I was hoping the taste would never run out.
Party on my mouth,
Party in my house,
So divine, so sweet,
I loved it,
I wanted it,
So this is what I was making,
So this is what I had been missing!

Jamie Edwards (11)
St Peter & St Paul CE Primary School, Bexhill-on-Sea

Beautiful Wonders

Mushroom
Like a spiralling tortoise shell
Mushroom
Sometimes tasty but sometimes deadly,
All shapes and *sizes!*

Aloe vera
As smooth as silk,
But as strong as oak,
As green as grass,
But as sharp as a sword.

Thomas Routley (10)
St Peter & St Paul CE Primary School, Bexhill-on-Sea

Wonders Of Nature

A mushroom shaped like a spiral
Whiteness, like milk from a coconut.

Bark like a map
An orchid angel
Pansies like kiwi fruits
Rhododendron
A princess surrounded by her strong healthy guards.

The Queen's cup is a beautiful shooting star,
Surrounded by a bright green soft pillow.

Gerbera like an overlapping firework,
An amazing sight to see.

Forget-me-not, a bunch of flowers
Glowing as the sun goes down.

Giant snowflakes suspended
A frozen Christmas tree
Dull, white as the sun disappears.

Nature is beautiful,
What a wonderful world we live in.

Hannah Mabb (11)
St Peter & St Paul CE Primary School, Bexhill-on-Sea

Beautiful World

Pansy, like a small, bright, yellow sun,
Mushroom, like a spiral twisting in mid-air,
Begonia, like a transparent tadpole's egg,
Aloe vera like a juicy kiwi, ripe and sweet,
Rough bark like a dinosaur's body,
Queen's cup, as white as milk.
Our beautiful world.

Greg Thompson (10)
St Peter & St Paul CE Primary School, Bexhill-on-Sea

Mouse

I, the weak creature,
Am like a newborn child.
I'm as afraid of you
As you are of me.
Just think of me as king of the timid.

I, a mouse,
Rule the scared.
I have to find your house.
I find you and give you disease.

I, a disease carrier,
Will try not to leave
Any proof of my visits.

I, a mouse
Roam my forest.

Hannah Sibson (10)
Shinewater Primary School, Eastbourne

Wind

The sound of it is getting closer,
It's coming for its revenge,
It's howling for its destiny,
Blowing harder and harder.

It may even get harder,
Who knows?
I do, I'm sitting here under my cover,
Listening to the sound.
I look out of the window
And there he is, outside.

Jodie Pescott (11)
Shinewater Primary School, Eastbourne

Fire

Fire is a burning sun, destroying forests and trees,
Fierce, indestructible, killing.
A beast destroying everything in its way,
Passing out deadly smoke.
I feel frightened for I know if it touches me,
I will surely die.
It's frightening, scary to know it's coming
Towards you and your family.
Fire is deadly,
If it touches your family or friends
Or even enemies,
They will die in a wink of an eye.
Fire is angry.
A red demon who rises once more.

Kadie Cox (10)
Shinewater Primary School, Eastbourne

Storm

A storm is a lion releasing its mighty roar of thunder.
A dark shadow has fallen upon the Earth;
Volcanoes are erupting,
Earthquakes are starting,
Ships are sinking,
Planes are crashing,
This is only the beginning!

God is in a temper,
Unleashing his bad mood,
Blaming it on the world
When will they ever learn?

Harry Mannel (11)
Shinewater Primary School, Eastbourne

Snow

Snow is like your guardian angels
Coming down to play with you.
They drift down from their homes in the clouds.
As they arrive, they huddle together
So that they get here without being eaten.

As they drift down
They glow and look like snow.
Their queen sends them down
To check on you and make sure you're alright.

Sophie Edwards (11)
Shinewater Primary School, Eastbourne

Lion

I, king of all lions
Rule the universe.
No animal has such sharp teeth,
Daggers.
Piercing anyone who challenges me,
My skills in combat are one of a unique sort
As I choose and kill my prey.
My brain can outwit anyone or anything.
I am king of the world.

Daniel McManus (10)
Shinewater Primary School, Eastbourne

Colourful - Cinquain

Rainbow
Colourful stripes
Only when rain has stopped
Brings joy to people's hearts and souls
Rainbow.

Rachel O'Reilly (11)
Shinewater Primary School, Eastbourne

Peacock

I, king of all birds,
Am the most beautiful bird of all time.
My eyes, you've seen them,
They're just the most beautiful eyes you've ever seen,
My secret,
You don't know.
Well my spying red oval eyes,
Sitting on the back of feathery tail
Are spying on whatever steps on
Or touches this world.
My world.

Laura Davies (10)
Shinewater Primary School, Eastbourne

Volcano

The volcano,
Large, immense, mighty and powerful.
Like a spacecraft preparing to take off at any time.
Like a paint bottle which bursts open whenever it wants.
Makes me feel small
Like a tiny fly no one can see.
The volcano
Reminds me how our lives are in danger!

Alex Trussell (11)
Shinewater Primary School, Eastbourne

Sea Horse - Cinquain

Sea horse
Plays with fish friend.
Prancing through the seabed,
Sleeping happily on seashore,
Snoozing.

Sofia Rebaudo (10)
Shinewater Primary School, Eastbourne

Ghost

A ghost is the power of your dreams,
Waiting in the depths of your homes.
It flies at midnight, every single night,
Always taking and killing souls.

Why the ghost does this
We don't know!
But all we know is they're in your
Houses, right at this moment.
Always waiting to take and kill your soul!

Elise Vincent (11)
Shinewater Primary School, Eastbourne

Snowflake

Snowflake,
A thick piece of stained glass,
Beautiful, icy, glittering.
Like a crystal, showing its beauty,
Like an angel falling from the sky.
It makes me feel ugly,
Like a toad no one dares to look at.
Snowflake,
Reminds us how pretty life can be.

Riva Cassidy (10)
Shinewater Primary School, Eastbourne

Earthquake

What is an earthquake?
An earthquake is a giant.
Jumping up and down
Because he's angry at his wife
For selling his favourite stuff.

William Upton (10)
Shinewater Primary School, Eastbourne

Rainbow

A rainbow is a piece of God
A splash of nature.
Every brightening colour
That'll wake you up in the morning
With a great big smile.

Rainbows are angels dancing through the sky.
They give life to flowers;
They're made from jelly beans and Smarties.
Children will laugh and stay watching it,
Till it fades away onto the horizon.

Charlotte Webb (10)
Shinewater Primary School, Eastbourne

Water Snake

Thou slithers in the darkest depths
Of the ocean floors
Waiting for your prey.
With one bite, it's dead.
Thou art poisonous.
We will not live more than a week
Around here!

Amy Drummond (11)
Shinewater Primary School, Eastbourne

Noises - Cinquain

Thunder
Making noises
With the rain and lightning
In a storm together they are
Daunting!

Ellen Curd (11)
Shinewater Primary School, Eastbourne

Snowflake

A snowflake is dust,
Dust that has fallen off a fairy's wand.
Sparkly glitter fallen into God's garden.
A magical place where you live.
Hold a snowflake in your hand,
Let it melt and you'll be filled with joy.
Invite the fairy into your home,
Look outside and see the crystal snowflakes falling down.
Some are pearls and some are diamonds,
Don't feel greedy or it will disappear in the palm of your hands.
Let it fall,
Let it snow.

Popi Begum (11)
Shinewater Primary School, Eastbourne

Comet

A comet is waiting
Before the depths of the world,
Waiting to lash down at any moment.
And then it does
Killing anything in its way
By leaving a stream of polluted gas
That poisons anyone that sniffs it in.
It looks depressed,
As if it knows it will destroy itself
As well as everyone else,
Not afraid.

Thomas Avery (11)
Shinewater Primary School, Eastbourne

Eagle

I am the toughest bird in the world,
I have never been defeated by any other kind.
My army will destroy any predators
On my land.

My wings are a cape over my land.
I soar through the air in search of my supper.
I sleep in a hole in a cliff
To look upon my world when I awake.

I will stay and fight for my land,
Destroy any armada that tries to take over my universe,
My beak, the ultimate weapon.

Christopher Mockford (10)
Shinewater Primary School, Eastbourne

Thunder

The Devil thrashes around restlessly,
He's furious that he's been beaten
By his enemy, God.

The demons are sent
Up to the sky.
Where they cast spells of gold and yellow,
Causing mayhem on the earth below.

Trees are scared
That they will be hit.
People rush inside, as the spells chase after them.

Ashley Green (10)
Shinewater Primary School, Eastbourne

Snowflake

An angel is floating down to make your wish,
God has sent them from His wand.
It's killing the flowers,
The angels are cold.
You can play outside with them,
Angels are bullets that have come to play.

The summer rises,
The angels melt.
Now they're on their way home,
Floating into the sky.

Charlotte Wilkins (11)
Shinewater Primary School, Eastbourne

Angel

Angel
Created by God.
Beautiful, kind, soft,
Like a snowflake touching your nose.
Like Heaven is coming to Earth.
It makes me feel important,
Like a queen going on holiday.
Angel.
Reminds us how beautiful we all are.

Sadie Cain (10)
Shinewater Primary School, Eastbourne

Levitating Leaves

A scarlet red leaf levitated,
And leapt into the wind.
It danced like a ballerina,
But then it went calm again
And it pirouetted down to rest.

James McCrone (10)
Sidlesham Primary School, Chichester

Fireworks

F ireworks sparkle, crackle and dazzle
I lluminating the night sky
R oaring rockets shoot up very high
E xcited children everywhere
W hoosh, bang, whizz they go
O range, green, red, so many colours
R oman candles glow in the dark
K aleidoscopic patterns for us to see
S parklers like shooting stars.

Stephanie Golder (11)
Sidlesham Primary School, Chichester

What Are The Clouds?

The clouds are white splodges of paint
spilt on a blue plate.
They are white flowers in
blue meadows.
They are white baubles on
blue Christmas trees.
They are white kittens asleep
with their heads tucked under their
furry tummies on blue cushions.

Chloe Russell-Sharp (7)
Sidlesham Primary School, Chichester

White Waves

What are white waves?
The white wave is like a white horse,
Swimming in the deep blue sea.
It's like ice cream in a dark blue bowl.
They're like white pots on a dark blue shelf.
They're white suns in a dark blue sky.
It's a white cat in a big blue basket.

Rachael Manley (8)
Sidlesham Primary School, Chichester

Autumn Come, Autumn Go

The summer has a smiley reign,
That has now gone away.
As the wild wind
Blows the tree boughs bare.

The changing leaves
Dance in the breeze.
As the birds fly away
Until another day.

As the trees get stripped
Of their leaves.
A stronger wind blows
As autumn gets pushed away.

But autumn says, 'No!'
And pushes back.
The wild wind pushes him
As he whistles.

'Winter wants to come!'
We say goodbye autumn
And he leaves the trees bare
With not one dancing leaf.

Victoria Lamb (10)
Sidlesham Primary School, Chichester

Kittens

Kittens are naughty,
Kittens are fun
And they act so cute when they're fed.
They love to be stroked,
They purr like a sewing machine,
Kittens are naughty,
Kittens are fun,
And when it's the evening they
Will lay in the shadow of the setting sun.

Lizzie Forbes (9)
Sidlesham Primary School, Chichester

You Little Monkey

My mum said
I was behaving
like a little monkey,
So I climbed
onto the sofa
and started swinging
on the door.

When she told me to stop,
I made chattering noises
and pretended
to scratch my armpits.

I refused
to talk properly
until teatime,
when all I got
was a plate of nuts
and a banana.

So I decided
to stop monkeying about.
But I think my
dad is a monkey and
my brother is a chimp.
Now that really is true!

Freddie Pickering (8)
Sidlesham Primary School, Chichester

Cats

Cats are thin, cats are fat,
Cats are white and cats are black.

Cats are *big,* cats are small
But the best cat of all is . . .
Ginger, my big, fat,
Cuddly *cat.*

Anna Rawlinson (9)
Sidlesham Primary School, Chichester

Playground Fun

Skipping, jumping
Oh so high,
Try not to trip
For you might cry.

Running, dashing
Here and there,
A peer in the pond
I wonder what's there?

Maybe a frog,
Maybe a fish.
I'll drop in a penny
And make a wish.

Under the hedge
To fetch our ball,
Don't lean too far
Or else you'll fall.

I look under a log
To see what's there,
A fat old toad
With an ugly stare.

I pick it up
And grasp it tight
I showed the headmaster
And gave him a fright.

I didn't mean to scare him
It was all a muddle,
He took a step back
And fell in a puddle.

Sian Louise Tunnell (9)
Sidlesham Primary School, Chichester

The Misty Morning

Outside turned to mist,
The sun was pale and weak,
The birds squawking everywhere,
The dew glitters like diamonds.
The sun was peeking through the trees,
With colours of orange and gold.
The cold nips at my ears,
The buds are developing.
The spiky trees reach up,
Mist fills the air.
The air is cold and misty,
Shadows of people in the mist.
In the shade it's colder,
The screech of birds in my ear.
Ivy covers the trees,
Mist, what great secrets you hold!

Abbie-Rose Curbison (8)
Sidlesham Primary School, Chichester

From The Town To The Sea

I'd love to live near the sea
My brother Leighton, my mum and me.
We used to live in a busy town
Where everybody rushed around.
There was no beach,
There was no sun.
There were no waves
We had no fun.
Then one day we moved away,
I was sad but now I'm happy
Every day.

Beau Sullivan (9)
Sidlesham Primary School, Chichester

The Colours Of The Rainbow

Red is a sunset
Orange is a red blazing sun,
Yellow is a field full of corn,
Green is springtime
Blue is a summer's sky
Indigo is a night's sea
Violet is a beautiful flower.

Jasmine Coppin (10)
Sidlesham Primary School, Chichester

Stars

Stars
sparkling
on a winter's
night. The wonder
of Heaven. So clear and
so bright. Fairy lights
twinkling on my Christmas
tree, share a message of joy
with you and me.

Tom Curbison (10)
Sidlesham Primary School, Chichester

My Funny Family

My brother is annoying,
My sister is just fine,
My mum is just shouting all the time,
My dad is alright, just a little weak,
But all he likes doing is playing hide-and-seek,
Libby is just funny as she normally is,
Then there's Sam, so sweet!

Shannon Williams (9)
The Oaks Primary School, Crawley

Man U Rule

M anchester United rule,
A rsenal are bad,
N orwich are OK,

U nited are the best, they beat all the rest

R eal Madrid are good,
U nited, United are the best in town,
L ay off shots are good,
E veryone should support Man U.

Jason Harrold (10)
The Oaks Primary School, Crawley

Football

F ootball is fun,
O h football is my best sport,
O h football keeps you fit,
T he best team is Man United.
B oots help you play,
A very good coach makes a good team,
L ay off, free kick you might score,
L osers always shake hands.

Adam Laker (10)
The Oaks Primary School, Crawley

In The Playground

In the playground I hear some noise,
In the playground there are always toys,
I hear the swings.
But I always hear them
Kind of things!

Rebecca Leach (9)
The Oaks Primary School, Crawley

Jumping Dolphins In The Sea

Jumping dolphins in the sea, splash, splash, splat,
See them twirling and dancing upon the water's mat.

See the little light they shine, what a pretty sight!
Don't you want to ride upon a little dolphin's back?

As they ride in the sea, see the fishes as they sparkle
And shine.

With the colours of a rainbow red, yellow and brown,
Look at it when the sun goes down with dolphins
Jumping up and down.

Amberley Hillyard (9)
The Oaks Primary School, Crawley

The Sphinx

A horrid monster,
With a face of an ugly woman,
A body of a meat-eating lion,
Wings of a bold golden eagle,
Tail of a slimy snake.

You should be scared of this monster,
Be scared,
Be frightened,
If you wish.

Tonight will be a night where
Blood is drawn,
All you have to do is answer a riddle . . .

Emily Harman (9)
The Oaks Primary School, Crawley

The Stormy Night

The sea is a great big swimming pool,
As tough as ten cheetahs,
The sea that sways in the wind,
It was one night that I noticed the sky is black,
The thunder roars,
People shiver to the shivering shades of ashes,
I shiver in my covers on my bed,
I couldn't stand the noise,
I was too scared to even pick up my glass of milk.

Suddenly it all stopped,
An eagle came and gave me its good greetings,
That was lost in the second of time.

Benjamin Hillyard (7)
The Oaks Primary School, Crawley

Poem About My Cat

My cat called Moggy came in my room last night,
I was amazed at the sight,
He was purring like mad
But he was sad,
He had no food in his bowl,
A toy in my room fell,
I think it was my doll,
I said to Mog, 'You poor little soul,'
I gave him some meat,
He sat in his seat and
He just went to sleep,
I went back to bed and said,
'Goodnight Moggy.'

Sarah Nash (9)
The Oaks Primary School, Crawley

Cat

The black cat yawns,
Opens her jaws,
Stretches her legs
And shows her claws.

Then she gets up
And stands on four
Long, stiff legs
And yawns
Some more.

She shows her sharp teeth,
She stretches her lips,
The end of her tongue,
Turns up at the tip,
Lifting herself on her delicate toes,
She arches her back as high as it goes.

She lets herself down,
With particular care
And pads away,
With her tail in the air.

Heidi Walker (9)
The Oaks Primary School, Crawley

In My Twisting Dream

In my twisting, turning dream,
My eyes go all a-gleam,
Around my head whilst I'm in bed,
My dreams, my dreams, my dreams.

Sometimes they're good,
Sometimes they're bad,
But then I go and cuddle my dad,
My dreams, my dreams, my dreams.

Hannah Traylen (9)
The Oaks Primary School, Crawley

My Teacher

My teacher is kind,
And anyone's blind,
Not to notice the magic,
Of this gadget,
To have such a lovely teacher.

She has beautiful short hair,
And would win at a fair
Beauty contest,
And would you guess
That she's the *best*!

Now it's time for a lesson,
So I'll have a wonderful session,
I know I'm lucky,
Oh, and she wouldn't mind if you brought a ducky
Into her classroom!
She's the best!

Emily Mashiter (10)
The Oaks Primary School, Crawley

Rainbow Bear

I am the bear of the ocean,
I am the bear of my whiteness,
I am the bear of the Arctic,
I shimmer and glitter on the moon,
I never stop until it's noon,
I float and glide along the sea,
And I like laying there watching the bumblebees,
I'm a bear with a big belly,
When I get scared my legs turn to jelly,
I gulp and gulp until I'm stuffed,
I try to keep myself fit but I get too puffed.
I am rainbow bear.

Stacey Truss (9)
The Oaks Primary School, Crawley

I Was Going On A Journey To The Afterlife

I was running to the afterlife,
Whizzing down the winding path
And going very fast.

I was going on a journey,
But suddenly I smelt a smell,
A really bad smell,
In front of me
Was a terrible monster made of slime,
Flowing in the breeze.

I was going on a journey
And suddenly I saw a petalled golden,
Overjoyed flower dancing in the sunlight,
Dancing the waltz.

I was going on a journey,
When I touched a thing,
Dangling from a tree,
I think it was a gappy skeleton,
I didn't quite see.

I was going on a journey,
When meanwhile I saw a young man
On a bench
Reading the news,
Then I saw a mouse behind a bush.

I was going on a journey,
But then I came across
A sleeping guardian wearing pink PJs,
I tiptoed past him,
'Phoo!' I said.

I was going on a journey,
When I came across a jabberwocky
Holding a deadly knife!
I was going on a journey to the afterlife.

Alice Alderson (8)
The Oaks Primary School, Crawley

Manchester United

M anchester United are the best,
A ll the players are the best,
N o more teams have got a chance.

U nhappy the away fans are,
N ow we're going to be the best,
I know that they're going to win because we
                        got our best team out,
T en is the number we all know, for the great
                   Van Nistelrooy will score a goal,
E ven more goals will be scored by number nine,
                   from the great Wayne Rooney,
D own in the changing room there's a great cheer for
                   the victory of the Red Devils.

Scott Lumley (10)
The Oaks Primary School, Crawley

Dinosaurs

D evastating dinosaurs stomp through the woods,
I guanodon has thumbs up,
N o man has ever seen them,
O h man, how big are dinosaurs?
S pinosaurus are the biggest in the whole world,
A nklesaurs are the armour plated ones,
U nsafe when you come across those big creatures,
R aptors are the fastest runners and killers in the world,
S pinosaurs have the biggest mouth and teeth.

Oliver Smith (10)
The Oaks Primary School, Crawley

Curious Kitty

Sleek, sly, slow, silent,
Cat creeps through the night,
Onto a wall, under a hedge,
Out into cold moonlight,
Silver claws on silver paws,
Jump up on a wall,
Here she sits and sees her friends,
Oh no they start to call!
Poor little kitty, now it rains,
Under a bridge, she's safe again.
Poor little cat, now it snows,
An icy wind begins to blow,
Run little kitty, run down the track,
Up your stairs and safely back.

Jodie Pemberton (9)
The Oaks Primary School, Crawley

War Poetry

The sound of men screaming,
The water is up to my knees,
The smell of poo and dead people,
Holding a bottle of water too scared to move.

The smell of gunfire fills my nose,
The sound of gunfire in my ear,
Waiting for the enemy,
Waiting just waiting,
The gun laughed as I shot a man in the head.

Seeing the dead body at my feet,
Hearing the body falling on the ground,
Holding dead people in my hands,
The blood all over my hands and clothes.

Harry Hills (11)
Tollgate Community Junior School, Eastbourne

Shooting In The Battlefields

The smell of urine disintegrating the gravel,
The bodies laying in their own blood,
The coldness freezing my body as I pull the *trigger,*
My clothes dripping of water and mud as I'm in the trench,
Throat dry, as I wait for the enemy,
The smell of smoke shoots up my nose,
Trees falling and hitting my friends,
Picking up frozen, dead bodies off the cold gravel,
Feeling heartbroken as my friends fade away,
I can see guns next to dead bodies,
The smell of rotten bodies.

Tyla Hobbs (11)
Tollgate Community Junior School, Eastbourne

My War Poem!

The smell of urine as I sit in the slushy trench,
My throat's dry as I wait for the enemy,
Feeling angry and sad as I see my friends lying in pain,
My head's spinning as I lay in the dark, dismal trench.

I feel sick as I see my friends lying in their own blood,
I'm just wishing so much that this war would be over,
I feel like my head's going to burst if I stay in this trench any longer.

The smell of rotten bodies spinning around in my head,
I can feel my heart thumping inside my chest,
I see my fellow soldiers collecting the bodies,
I'm wondering if they'll ever collect mine.

I see my friends and family lying helpless,
I wish I were in their position,
I hear an innocent cry, then I realise it's me -
I've been hit!

Katy Spokes (10)
Tollgate Community Junior School, Eastbourne

My War Poem

Feeling sad as many of my close friends lie in agony,
Wishing I were in their position,
At least that way I wouldn't have to face this,
This horrible country, Germany!
Cold and lonely as the fierce wind blows
The urine and dirt all over my face,
Hearing both countries pull the trigger and
Here comes the death!

Did, did I get him?
Hope so, then at least that's one less German to
Worry about,
Although it's done and over with I feel guilty and
Broken-hearted,
Should I pull the trigger? No I can't,
My country is in danger, I must,
Bang!

Oh no, bodies are dropping into the mud in this dirty,
Scrummy trench,
Argh! I can't take it anymore,
No, it can't be him,
Please help me, I'm in major pain.

Feeling proud and wondering whether or not
You should have done it,
Will I see my family again?
Oh I do miss them so very much . . .
Bang!

Harley Buckwell (11)
Tollgate Community Junior School, Eastbourne

The Sun

The sun setting in the sky.
The sparkling sun shining like a star.
Shimmering, sizzling and setting in the sky.
The sensational sun shining in the sky.

Nadia Alam (9)
Tollgate Community Junior School, Eastbourne

In The Trench

The horrific stench of death hovers above your head,
You can hear gunfire,
Non-stop talking,
And the slushing of muddy water under your grubby boots.

Crystal-like tears fall from your eyes as you collect
The bodies of your fallen comrades.

You can smell burning and you can hear whistling
Of bombs overhead,
You have numb fingers,
But you can just pull your gun out of its sheath,
You peer over your trench ready to blast a German soldier,
Your gun is at the ready but your guilt and fear
Has overcome bravery and you sink back down into your trench.

You peek back over your trench once more,
This time your bravery has risen and you are ready to fire,
When you hear a loud *bang* and the trickling of blood
You sway your head from side to side to see who has been hit
Suddenly you fall onto your knees as you realise it is you,
Everything goes black, you fall further,
Now you are lying on the ground, there are loud voices all around,
Then nothing . . .

Ryan Dowding (11)
Tollgate Community Junior School, Eastbourne

The Sun

The sparkling sun shines down onto the sapphire sea,
While scaly sea lions swim to seek sight of sardines,
The scorching sun stands out as the stunning seagulls
Swoop up shellfish, struggling in the sand and people
Sunbathe leaving sandals on the seashore.

Tom Seath (10)
Tollgate Community Junior School, Eastbourne

Terrifying Trenches

We are cramped in a confined space,
The air grips its hands around my
Throat strangling me, strangling me.
Souls fly around disorientated in this
Miscellaneous world.
My throat is obstructed by a thick reeking gas.

Numbness drowns my hands as I wait for
A soldier to appear,
I hear my heart palpitating in this eerie atmosphere,
Remorse creeps over me as I let out a burst
Of death, burst of death,
Pictures replay through my mind of people dying,
Like a battered cinema track.

Chloe Humphreys (10)
Tollgate Community Junior School, Eastbourne

Shelter

S quash in-between the side,
H ear a bomb,
E ars listen as a plane crashes,
L ook outside house bombed,
T he siren goes for all clear,
E veryone comes out,
R ed fire we see being calmed down.

Kiaya Pike (10)
Tollgate Community Junior School, Eastbourne

Snow

The slippery, soft, slushy stuff falls to the ground.
Sensational snow sinking slowly.
Snow silently, slowly, sliding to the soft ground.
Slippery, sloppy snow falling to the ground.

Matthew Collett (10)
Tollgate Community Junior School, Eastbourne

The Tornado

The terrible, thrashing tornado
trashes theatres and taxis.
The tall, tangling tornado
tears theme parks, tents and towns
until only tarmac is left.

Harry Brabham (9)
Tollgate Community Junior School, Eastbourne

What I Could Hear

My mum tried to calm me down,
The boom of the bomb over the road,
The crash of the aeroplane being clattered by the guns,
The drop of the tear from my eye as I hear people screaming,
As I only can wait and hope for mercy,
As I sit in this dark, dismal shelter,
There's not much room, but enough,
Just enough
Then a hum, hum, hum
Then silence
Boom!
The shelter's dented
The Germans are vigorous to win
But we can't give in
Can we?

Bayan Fenwick (11)
Tollgate Community Junior School, Eastbourne

The Stars

The stars are smashed crystal floating in the sky
They are shattered glass on a black sea.
The stars are fairy lights on a Christmas tree.
They are snowdrops dropped from Heaven.
The stars are sugar floating in black coffee.

Amy Mugridge (10)
Vale First & Middle School, Worthing

My Life As A Weed

When I was young I wanted to wriggle around
It wasn't much fun being underground
Every time I saw a worm
It really made me squirm.
I just wanted to have lots of fun
So I decided to grow towards the sun
Up, up, up, I grew
Just nobody knew
That I was so lonely down there
And needed some fresh air.
I looked up at the sky
And watched the birds fly by.
I saw a kite
I knew I was right
To grow as tall as I could
Like most seeds should.
I got very green
And then could be seen
When a man came along
And stabbed me with a prong.
Now I don't want to be a weed
How I wish I was still a seed.

Martin Brooks (8)
Vale First & Middle School, Worthing

Dolphins

Shimmering in the water,
A flash of silver blue.

They skim through the ocean,
Then disappear from view.

I think I see a dolphin's head
Peeking out from the water
But I know it's not just the foam from the sea.

Daniel Parkman (8)
Vale First & Middle School, Worthing

I'm A Little Bumblebee

I'm a little bumblebee
Buzzing in a tree,
I stung someone
On their knee.

I'm a little bumblebee
I stung someone's leg
And when I stung them
They dropped an Easter egg!

I hibernate in the winter
In my little hole
And buzz out in the springtime
And once I stung a mole.

I'm a little bumblebee
Sitting on a cat,
I'm a very scared bumblebee
Being chased and being trapped in a hat.

I'm a very sad bumblebee
Feeling sorry for the things I've stung,
I managed to get out of the hat
And now I won't sting anyone!

Verity Wakeling (7)
Vale First & Middle School, Worthing

Hamsters

All the hamsters, furry and cute
With their tiny feet, twitchy noses
And the way they do their little poses.
Their different shades of fur,
I will love them forever.
They are so, so sweet
They are the cutest pets you'll ever meet!

Laura Edgoose (10)
Vale First & Middle School, Worthing

School Subjects

I really like PE
It's very simple you see.
You jog and you skip
You fall and you trip
And there is a much fitter me.

Maths isn't so great
A subject that I really hate
You don't have fun,
You do a sum
And end up just writing the date.

In English you have to indent
It's got to make some sense
If it does not,
The teacher will stop
And ask me just what I meant.

Lisa Whiting (9)
Vale First & Middle School, Worthing

Mysterious Monsters

Children think monsters are myths and not true.
Well my friend, that is not true, this whole world has got ghosts.

Green ghosts, defending Dracula, vicious vampires,
Frankenstein is my friend. They haunt woods,
Scare you, even make you have a heart attack.

Just because you do not see them it does not mean they are fake.
No one sees them fall in a lake.

That is true because I am the creator
Of all *monsters!*

Emily Cartwright (9)
Vale First & Middle School, Worthing

Fun At The Park

It was a nice, bright, sunny day and three friends wanted to play.
They decided to go to the park to play
They took some sandwiches and drink, ready for their picnic.
They played happily in the sun and decided to eat their lunch at 1.00.
Their aunt came to see if they were all right.
They played on the swings, the see-saw
Then they went for a ride on the roundabout.
Then on the slide. They sat down and were talking about school
How they were doing and what their favourite subject was at school.
After a while they thought they would go home and ask their mum
                                             for an ice cream.
When they got home their mum gave them an ice cream out
                                             of the freezer.
Jenny's mum asked Sally and Maria if they would like to stay
                                             to tea and then watch some TV.
Then Jenny rang up the parents and said she would take them
                                             home after tea.
So they all had a very good day and they went to bed.

Natalia Gargaro (9)
Vale First & Middle School, Worthing

A Christmas Poem

Sitting round the warm fire,
Opening presents to your desire,
Sending cards along the way,
Opening them on Christmas Day,
When the world begins to get white,
It really is a beautiful sight,
Sitting on sleds while going down hills,
It really is a great big thrill,
When Christmas is nearly over,
I can pick flowers like bluebells and clover.

Siobhan Stanbridge (9)
Vale First & Middle School, Worthing

I Found A Way

I found the time
And the place,
Just to say it to your face.

I don't know why,
But I will find out,
To disguise my face
In a way.

Not sure what with,
But still believe,
I'll be with you
So do not weep.

Georgia Linfield (10)
Vale First & Middle School, Worthing

Snow

Snow, snow, cold as ice
Thick as glue, white and nice.
As the snowflakes fall
And I walk home from school,
As I am going the leaves are blowing.
The snow is glistening
And I am listening
To the wind while it blows.
The snow goes crunch, crunch
Under my feet.
The sun comes out
And the snow turns to sleet.

Danielle Rogers (11)
Vale First & Middle School, Worthing

The Sea

A velvet blanket
A frothy tea
A huge swimming pool
For you and me

But think about it
What is in this beautiful sea?
We pollute it
You and me

Beneath the waves
Where no one can see
Rubbish and sewage
We've done that
You and me

The world's a big dustbin
That's the sea
What have we done
You and me?

Elizabeth Saxony (11)
Vale First & Middle School, Worthing

My Mum

My mum is really cool
She's really, really great
She doesn't have many rules
But she has loads of mates
She's nice all the time
She likes lots of things but not lime
So if you want to see the best mum in the world
Come round to my house
And we'll have a whirl!

Sophie Baker (9)
Vale First & Middle School, Worthing

My Family

My dad is a busy worker
He's up in London all day.

My sister is annoying
But she really is the best.

My mum is . . . well the greatest
She cooks the dinner
When we come home from school.

My family is spectacular though
The best of the best.

Rebecca Lewis (11)
Vale First & Middle School, Worthing

Dreamworld Verse

Nobody can tell what the dream holds
You're feeling drowsy, going to sleep
But the secrets the dreams behold they will keep
You tug the sheets over yourself in bed
The pillow comforts your head
You hope the sun will rise very soon
And that the daylight will devour the moon.

Adam Fitchett (9)
Vale First & Middle School, Worthing

Wizzy The Ant

I'm Wizzy the ant,
I'm silent and small,
I'm part red, part brown,
I have a black spot on my right back leg
And I stumble over the anthill all day long,
But one day I will be Wizzy the queen ant.

Stephanie Parkman (10)
Vale First & Middle School, Worthing

Sad
(For Rose Elsie Roberts)

Sadness - why are you here?
Why do you haunt me?
Why are you always so near?

I long to smile, to laugh out loud
To feel rays of sunshine and not tears of a cloud
And yet with sadness comes memories that are mine,
That I keep with me, small moments of time.

Frances Roberts (10)
Vale First & Middle School, Worthing

Crisps

Crisps are long,
Crisps are short,
Crisps come in any shape or sort.
I like crisps,
So do you,
Maybe I can make them just right for you.

Becky Potiphar (10)
Vale First & Middle School, Worthing

Candle Poem

My candle is beautiful gold
With a flame so bright
It will last twelve nights
It burns in a room of silver
For royalty maybe
But definitely for you and me

Chloe Slaughter (9)
Vale First & Middle School, Worthing

Trip To The Moon

The moon is a place of great mystery
You can't get to it by jumping or climbing a tree
But using a spacecraft you've got to be brave
Wear big spacesuits, your life they will save

If you ever go venturing up in space
It really is a mysterious place
It's for those who are brave, daring with skill
To go up into space you have to have will

Because if you don't it'll be very dull indeed
Pressing big buttons and travelling at speed
And when you get there you're mostly alone
The glare of the sun, the low key drone

Of the cameras watching your every move
It's dark and dull on the cold, lonely moon
And stare down at the Earth covered in white
The clouds covering the Earth with all their might

So now your time on the moon is soon at an end
Left at the right star, left round the bend
You're nearly home, your family awaits
To see you come home, it must be great

So now you are landing safe and well
Now on your space trip you have time to dwell
On the fact that you went up to the moon
Now it's over and done, so quickly, so soon.

Jessica Gilbert-McHugh (10)
Vale First & Middle School, Worthing

The Arctic Polar Bear

The Arctic polar bear with a coat so white
Standing in the snow they look so bright.

The Arctic polar bear eats fish as a dish
But would rather have a seal for a tastier meal.

The Arctic polar bear is very, very furry
If you see a few they could look rather blurry.

The Arctic polar bear has a little cub
If you were to see it you would want to give its fur a gentle rub.

The Arctic polar bear and her little cub
You'd better beware as they wouldn't want to share their tasty grub.

The Arctic polar bear
The Arctic polar bear.

Jasmine Street (10)
Vale First & Middle School, Worthing

Flint Cinquain

Jagged,
Rays of silver,
Deadly sharp, hard-wearing,
Piercing, cold, spiky and dazzling,
Ancient.

Rebecca Offer (11)
Vale First & Middle School, Worthing

Flint Cinquain

Jet-black
As old as time
Prehistoric mystery
Impenetrable . . . ashen stone
Ageless.

Rosalind Frayard-Smith (11)
Vale First & Middle School, Worthing

My Mum

My mum is really kind,
My mum is really caring.

My mum lets me do anything,
My mum lets me sing.

She is the bestest mum
In the world.

I would not change her,
Nor would she change me.

Rachel Rooke (10)
Vale First & Middle School, Worthing

Ignis' Fire

Flaming
Fieriest
Scarlet
Magma
Ribbons of golden fire tumble out
Blazing
Combustion
Inferno
Pyre
Blazing fire streaks out of his mouth
Happiness shows on his face
He dances about, joy in his smile
Then he lies down exhausted.

Georgina Morley (8)
Walberton & Binsted CE Primary School, Walberton

Ignis' Fire

The fiery, scalding, blistering fire
Which started with just a sparkle of light
How small it was, how light it was
Leaving its sparkles behind
The steaming, burning, sizzling fire was gulped into Ignis' mouth
He coughed and spluttered and sneezed,
But there was just a puff of smoke
The oppressive, sweltering, scorching fire burst out of his mouth
How amazed he was, how dazzled he was, that he found his fire!

Samuel Pierce (8)
Walberton & Binsted CE Primary School, Walberton

Ignis' Fire

First a friendly lick of flame trailing
A ruby-red strip shot out
Then a golden streamer unravelled itself
Steamy ribbons bounced out and grew fiery
Large, jagged, toasty flames
Burning, fiery ropes looped the night sky
A missile of blistering fire burst out like a scarlet magma eagle
Twisting and turning in the twinkling evening sky
With puffs of smoke surrounding Ignis.

James Baker (8)
Walberton & Binsted CE Primary School, Walberton

Ignis' Fire

It started off as a tiny flicker of fire,
A tiny puff of smoke turned into an amber blaze of fire
Suddenly a wonderful rage of fire rushed out.

A victorious, monstrous puff of overheated fire came out,
Suddenly a most enormous puff of fire settled in the night sky.

Joshua Harris (9)
Walberton & Binsted CE Primary School, Walberton

Devil Birth

In the circling dust of far-off lands, a desert lay
In the hot, hot sands, there raged a storm
In the raging storm, the Earth did crack
In that crack there blazed a fire
In that fire a puddle smoked
From that puddle a mist did whirl
And from that mist
Devil came!

Elizabeth Baxter (9)
Walberton & Binsted CE Primary School, Walberton

Phoenix Birth

In the rays of the sun of long ago
Underneath the sky stood a volcano . . .
Inside the volcano flowed blistering lava
In the lava there slept a boulder
In the boulder lay a cracked rock
Within the rock smouldered ashes
Out of the red-hot ashes
Phoenix came!

Alex Baker (8)
Walberton & Binsted CE Primary School, Walberton

Ignis' Fire

Out came a spark so bright and so smart
With a cough and a yawn a flame appeared
Then a golden ribbon waved
Suddenly a huge, blazing fire burst
Scarlet red, mango orange and sunny yellow
Ignis felt happy and victorious.

Megan Payne (9)
Walberton & Binsted CE Primary School, Walberton

Ignis' Fire

Ignis sighed, Ignis coughed, Ignis sneezed, Ignis blew
Then out came windy ribbons of fire
And roller coaster shaped balls of fire
Then an eruption of colourful fire burst out
Eventually Ignis' fire faded away
He slowly fell to the ground
Then slowly picked himself up and started again.

Edward Myers (9)
Walberton & Binsted CE Primary School, Walberton

Ignis' Fire

With a cough and a splutter,
With a yawn and a mutter,
He coughed his first little spark,
With a sting and a thump.
His heart went bump
And out came
A ribbon of flame
It danced around
Like streamers in a carnival.

Fire! Fire! Fire!
Out came a burst of mango, blood-red and
Orange blazing fire.

Poppy Crawford (8)
Walberton & Binsted CE Primary School, Walberton

Whirlpool

Round and round the whirlpool goes
Will it stop? Nobody knows!
Swirling and twirling and gushing and rushing
Spurting heavily, smashing and splashing
Round and round the whirlpool goes
Will it stop? Nobody knows!

Oliver Bower-Neville (9)
West Hove Junior School, Hove

Magnetic Anger

Magnetic anger ripe with rage
Pulling all mistakes up on stage
Magnetic anger fresh in criticism
Yanking each kid to a victim
Magnetic anger bright red
Forcing parents out of bed
Magnetic anger full of violence
Glaring into crowds of silence
Magnetic anger growing worse
Giving all a naughty curse
Magnetic anger from red to blue
Whacking animals with a mighty shoe
Magnetic anger never stopping
Giving you a huge shocking
Magnetic anger getting sleepy
Makes one last toddler very weepy
Magnetic anger snoring hard
Leaves people to their own backyard
Without disturbance
Well at least for an hour or two!

Isabella Millington (10)
West Hove Junior School, Hove

Fireworks

Fireworks, fireworks in the sky
Light them up and watch them fly
So many colours, burning so bright
In the night sky, it's a wonderful sight.
November the 5th is a special time
For it remembers Guy Fawkes -
Who committed a terrible crime.
Everyone is cheering with delight
For they're all having fun tonight.
Fireworks, fireworks, fireworks night.

Rushna Razak (10)
West Hove Junior School, Hove

Deep Down Inside Our Hearts . . .

Love is a strange thing
But we all know it's there
Deep down inside
Our hearts . . . love lays.

Love is a strong feeling
With kisses and laughter to share
Deep down inside
Our hearts . . . love lays.

Love cannot be explained,
But we all know it's important
Deep down inside
Our hearts . . . love lays.

Love is wonderful,
So magical when we're hugged,
Deep down inside
Our hearts . . . love lays.

Eva Zaninetti (10)
West Hove Junior School, Hove

A Grey Cloth

The fog
A grey, murky substance
Sliding through the countryside
Massive great hands
Prodding and poking
Hanging from cottages
Dripping from branches
Its long winding fingers
Grabbing and searching
It pays a visit to the town
Cuddling strangers like a great grey blanket
Wrapping up houses like Christmas presents
Fading, fading, fading away.

Aurora Miller (10)
West Hove Junior School, Hove

The Intruder With No Sound

Wind endlessly bounding through towns
Stealing hats off workers, kicking them down the street
The rubbish runs, careful not to be trampled by the tumbling
feet of the wind.
Wispy and white, but cunningly clear and invisible
Bustling through the towns like a cheetah into the countryside
Looting all the leaves and pilfering all the branches
Eventually coming to a tiring end, ready to pounce on its next victim.

Rhiannon Adams (11)
West Hove Junior School, Hove

Ocean

In my turquoise waves
There is love and hate
Joy and anger
I can sing
Or I can shout
I will hush a baby's cry
In spite I can kill
In love I can play
Racing seagulls
Either in happy leaps of aqua blue
Or cursing splashes of grey
I ride
Like a sea soldier
On white horses
Charge
Like one of the giant, grey monsters
In the reflections of my depths
Fly
Like a quick seagull
Up in the royal blue skies
I am your ocean!

Amy Pike (10)
West Hove Junior School, Hove

Bully Poem

Running, running
As fast as I can,
Wishing they would stop
Bullying me
My heart beats
Stop, stop, you're hurting me.

I tried to run,
They grabbed me against the wall
And *hurt me.*
My nose couldn't stop bleeding
And I couldn't stop pleading for
Help!

Jade Widdick (11)
West Hove Junior School, Hove

The Sun Shore

In the sun
I sit there
in the sun I am
the sand shore
glittering in the sunlight
shells in their shapes
crabs on the rocks
the sea with the gentle waves
I see it now
I see it now
in the sun
I sit there
in the sun I am.

Eleanor Cottingham (10)
West Hove Junior School, Hove

The Tornado

A tornado flies across the land
Like a blind bull charging
It rips up cars and houses
And flings them round and round
The tornado has an eye
An eye for trouble
But there's a heart in this eye
The heart is not ferocious
It is sad and calm
As it tries to find its way home.

Sammy Valder (10)
West Hove Junior School, Hove

Love On St Valentine's

St Valentine's Day has come,
Cards and presents,
From no one in particular.
Kisses and flowers,
For that special someone,
That we don't know,
Love all around
On St Valentine's.

Lucy Robinson (10)
West Hove Junior School, Hove

Haiku

Hallowe'en is near
The storms are never clear and
Winter's coming close.

Felix Boyce (9)
West Hove Junior School, Hove

The River

The river turning and whirling, crashing and splashing
It drifts round the bendy corner curling and swirling.
The sea bashes and clashes up onto the pebbly shore
We never know whether if it will return once more.
The river squirting and spurting, gushing and rushing
Round the corner lurking through the opening of the sea.
The sea smashing and crashing, swaying and spraying
Bashing and lashing, it bounces up into the air.

Summa Watson (9)
West Hove Junior School, Hove

Life Is A Meaning!

We are all made in our own different way
Clouds washing the sky away
In the end everyone has the truth
Everyone's different ways are filling the sky
With different shades
Life is drifting on
As everyone finds their meaning.

Lydia Pope (11)
West Hove Junior School, Hove

On The Beach

Hear the shells bang,
Hear a spade dig,
Hear the seagulls talk,
Hear a girl paddle in the sea,
Hear a dog bark at me,
Hear a man snoring,
Hear a dolphin splash.

Rebeka Howarth (7)
Wisborough Green Primary School, Wisborough Green

Wings

If I had wings
I would fly to the top of the sky and talk to God.

If I had wings
I would skim a morning lake and talk to fish.

If I had wings
I would breaststroke through the morning mist.

If I had wings
I would jump the moon and stars.

If I had wings
I would swim the desert and walk the sea.

Kwame Noye (9)
Wisborough Green Primary School, Wisborough Green

Trapped In A Car

Trapped in a car
Mum's in the market
She's just got out
But it seems like an hour.
Oh, I can't open the windows
It's all hot and sticky
I'm sweating
It's been two hours.
It is so hot
I'm losing my voice
I can see Mum
With an ice cream
I have licked it
It is so cool.

Connor Worrell (9)
Wisborough Green Primary School, Wisborough Green

Playtime

I am so bored
I need to get out to play
I'm stuck here in this hot, sticky library
Doing long, hard science and writing.
Having to think of a way to do an investigation
I wonder if she'll let me go to the toilet or get a drink
Why, oh why, do I have to be writing
When I could be playing cards and running around?
Oh no, now I have to do the investigation.
Wish me luck!
Ten minutes until play,
Five minutes,
Two minutes,
10, 9, 8, 7, 6, 5, 4, 3, 2, 1
I'm *free!*

George Gibson (9)
Wisborough Green Primary School, Wisborough Green

Aztec Warrior

He watched with fright
He set off for war
Hope, anger, hate
He was scared.

He sensed the war
He touched his head
His warm, watery, wet
Sweat trickling down.

He was scared
His body froze
He saw arrows
He felt blood.

Rachel Warwick (10)
Wisborough Green Primary School, Wisborough Green

Wings

If I had wings
I would jump and dive along with dolphins.

If I had wings
I would drop down with the raindrops.

If I had wings
I would fly to Australia and jump with kangaroos.

If I had wings
I would help a golden eagle to hunt his prey.

If I had wings
I would arrange the stars into a *'Go To Sleep'* sign
For children that are still awake.

If I had wings
I would glide along with the thin air.

If I had wings
I would fly to Australia and learn how to play a didgeridoo.

If I had wings
I would swim in the sky and dance above the sea
And walk over the clouds.

Laura Appleton (8)
Wisborough Green Primary School, Wisborough Green

On The Beach

On the beach I found
A crab who nipped my toe and ran.
I chased the crab and hit a rock
And started crying.
So I sat and watched the boats
And forgot about the crab.
Then I went home.

Henry Felton (7)
Wisborough Green Primary School, Wisborough Green

Wings

If I had wings
I would twirl around the aeroplanes, then drop from the sky.

If I had wings
I would go to the clouds and take some and come back down.

If I had wings
I would fly to the tops of houses and slide down the roof.

If I had wings
I would glide across the mountains and sledge down them.

If I had wings
I would soar over the hills and collect some flowers.

If I had wings
I would go to the stars and sit on the moon.

If I had wings
I would go to all sorts of shops and buy all sorts of things.

If I had wings
I would twirl around the world and find more friends.

Ailish Fowler (8)
Wisborough Green Primary School, Wisborough Green

The Warrior

I woke up
The rough, bare arms of the tree
Were wriggling their way through the air.
The sun had woken from her sleep
As I walked
She glistened wildly
I was nervous
I wondered what war would be like
Would it be vicious?
I walked
On the sandy paths of golden crystals.

Lucy Donovan (11)
Wisborough Green Primary School, Wisborough Green

Wings

If I had wings
I would fly round mountains and glide through cirrus clouds.

If I had wings
I would use the blueness as swimming pools
And dive through and hit the nice soft bottom.

If I had wings
I would play football with aliens and beat them 10-0.

If I had wings
I would search the universe and discover sympyreos.

If I had wings
I would fly into a hurricane
And twirl and twirl getting very dizzy indeed.

If I had wings
I would feel fabulous, I would swoop everywhere
It would be the best thing in the world for me.

Joey Calder Smith (8)
Wisborough Green Primary School, Wisborough Green

Aztec Warrior

He woke up to find the same tree growing old.
The sun rising and smiling at him in sadness
His jet-black hair was like horses running
The hot sand pulling him down with its burning hands.

The sweat running down his forehead was like snakes slithering
He was walking to war and his inside animal was taking over him
He walked like a proud cat
His eyes had the smile of a devil in them.

He died like a waterfall smashing through the water's surface
The sun's warm smile fell to a deadly rainfall
That same tree stayed tall and timeless.

Iona Spackman (10)
Wisborough Green Primary School, Wisborough Green

Aztec Warrior

As the warrior woke up
He saw the sun blazing down
His weapons lying on the ground
The sand sparkling
The grass in the distance sizzling
The animals galloping
The trees twisting and turning
The heat stole his energy
He cupped his hands
And poured freezing crystal water
Onto his jet-black hair
Onto his clothes
The perspiration dripping down his eyes
The head warrior coming
He got his weapons
And went to war.

Lauren Napper (10)
Wisborough Green Primary School, Wisborough Green

Aztec Warrior

As I woke up I saw the whispering tree wave down at me
I stood up and looked at the moon jump down
And the sun climb up into its place
I rowed across the blank, staring water
I felt the hot sand sink around my feet
My hair was a rough ocean, swirling in all directions
The sweat dripped
My cloak flapped in the breeze
Swirling,
Twirling,
As I ran into battle.

Paddy Fowler (10)
Wisborough Green Primary School, Wisborough Green

A Warrior

A silent, deep blue morning all around,
Broken only by the tramping of distant enemy soldiers on the ground.
The Aztecs awake preparing for war,
For pride they would fight, by sunrise they saw.
The warrior rose and tied up his raven-black hair,
He was used to the fierce heat so did not care.
He picked up his sharp spear and went to meet the Spanish,
The enemy marched on and the tension would not vanish.
The legions trudged on through the scorching, golden sand
A roar went up
Spears glinting
Guns loaded
Aztec army, once so strong and so proud
Gone
Barren, empty landscape.

Joely Santa Cruz (11)
Wisborough Green Primary School, Wisborough Green

The Warrior

I am a warrior
My skin brown with heat
My hair jet-black
Before this day
I was peacefully sleeping
Under the smiling moon
And the glistening stars
But now
The sun has an unhappy face
Today
I am going to war.

Oliver Luddy (10)
Wisborough Green Primary School, Wisborough Green

The Warrior

I open my eyes to tingling hair
The moon fading to nothing
I looked up at the sky
To find the sun smiling back at me
I wiped my brow with my hand
The sand wriggled like a snake beneath me
I stand up
I start walking along the burning sand
I stand tall, but my shadow is scared
The scorching sun beating down my back
My tunic stuck to my sticky skin
My soaked, jet-black hair lay against my boiling neck
My tanned, bronze skin is burning
My spear digs into my thigh and yet
It is my only friend
My only reassurance.

Georgina Marfe (10)
Wisborough Green Primary School, Wisborough Green

Waiting

As I lay there in the desert
Against the rocky tree
I was waiting for the woeful war
But it wasn't just me.

The landscape looked so lifeless
I could only go one way
To battle for my country
And fight all through the day.

I was ready for the fight
My heart knocking on the door
I stood there with the tribe
Just waiting for the war.

Ollie Howarth (10)
Wisborough Green Primary School, Wisborough Green

Autumn Leaves

The autumn leaves are twinkling in the sunset
All the leaves are covered in dew
There are streaks of lovely colours
Pinks and browny yellows.
A gust of wind comes
It twists the leaves around as they fall off the tree.
I watch them glide and flutter around
And land gently together on the dewy grass.
The morning mist is falling and still
Golden leaves in the chilly air, dying in the warm sun
More leaves gently swirl.
Red, greens and yellows.
A gentle breeze ruffles the fallen leaves up
A robin flutters down onto a branch,
Picks up a leaf
And flies away.

Alice Groves (10)
Wisborough Green Primary School, Wisborough Green

The Warrior

I woke up sitting at the feet of a tree
Leaning on its rough skin
I stood up
The bright sun rose
As I walked off to war
The tree stared and waved its branches
Its arms punching the air
My feet sank into the silky sand
I could see the tip of the temple.

Rosie Osmaston (10)
Wisborough Green Primary School, Wisborough Green

The Seaside

I see the waves splashing on the beach,
Seaweed coming up from the waves,
I love how the seagulls flap their wings,
The white horses are alive on the waves.

I love to squidge the anemones and see them open,
Hunting for crabs,
Looking for shells,
I can feel my feet sinking in the water.

Children playing on the beach,
The Atlantic Ocean springs into the sky
And is smashing on the rocks,
I love the salty sea,
A child climbing on rocks
As I leave I say goodbye.

Katie Wells (9)
Wisborough Green Primary School, Wisborough Green

The Warrior

I opened my eyes and could feel
The sun beating down on me
I could feel the tree crunch its leaves
When it swayed in the wind.

The tree had rough skin like an old man
I could feel the sweat dripping down my face
I could feel the sand burning my feet like a blazing fire
I could see the enemy charging over the hill.

Zachary Voaden (11)
Wisborough Green Primary School, Wisborough Green

On The Beach

The sea dancing,
The waves prancing,
Dolphins splashing with joy.
The squawk of seagulls,
Wild seagulls.
Collecting seashells as well as
Pebbles so smooth.
The sun so hot,
The smell of seaweed,
The noise of waves crashing onto the sand.
The sound of people stepping on the stones
People together, people on their own.
Mermaids splashing,
Sea swirling,
Sea sparkling.
Sea horses twirling
Footprints pressed in the sand.
No matter if the sand is dry or wet
It is still part of the land.

Isobel Dyer (7)
Wisborough Green Primary School, Wisborough Green

The Warrior

He awoke
He saw the tree's long, dry branches waving gently
Reassuring him
The sun smiled
As the smile faded he arose
Excited and scared
As his heart pounded
He stepped up
The dark, gloomy thought of war
He saw the warriors rise from the fiery sand.

Jonathan Maunders (10)
Wisborough Green Primary School, Wisborough Green

Listen To The Seashore

The waves going up and down across the shore,
Starfish and fish swimming in the sea,
Sand like silk.
Wind blowing sand everywhere.
Hear the seagulls making noises.
Listen to the tide coming towards you
Smell the salt in the sea.
See the pretty shells hiding in the sand,
Look at the people swimming by the shore.
Dogs just come from the sea shaking all over you.
Look at the mermaids sitting on the rocks.
See the dolphins twirling over the waves,
Smell the food from nearby
See adults getting tanned,
Listen to the crabs clicking their claws,
Look at people playing volleyball and football in the sand.

Edwina Lywood (7)
Wisborough Green Primary School, Wisborough Green

Aztec Warrior

I opened my eyes,
I saw the sun,
Its bright smile dazzled my eyes.
I felt the rough skin of an ancient tree on my back
I had thick, heavy armour on.
My jet-black, wispy hair blew in the wind.
My weapon close to my side
My shield on my arm
As thoughts ran through my head.
I was ready for war
Before I knew it, the horn blew
It was time.

Laura Mackinnon (11)
Wisborough Green Primary School, Wisborough Green

Aztec Warrior

He woke up under a tree
Standing up and stumbling against the bark
The tree skin was very rough
He was going back to war
The sun winked at him
The hot sand slithered away from his feet
His spear was his special friend
He glanced to the left
His heart pumping like a drum
His shaking knees fell to the ground.

Daniel MacDonald (10)
Wisborough Green Primary School, Wisborough Green

The Warrior

I woke up to feel a tree's rough skin on my face
I looked up to see its many arms and legs reaching out
As the morning sun awoke
The needles from its fiery glare struck the ground
As I stretched my stiffened legs
They sank into the sand
The thought hit me
The reality of what was about to happen.

Lucy Boxall (10)
Wisborough Green Primary School, Wisborough Green

Coughs And Colds - Haiku

You sniff and you cough
When you have these illnesses
It's annoying me.

Laura Parker (8)
Wisborough Green Primary School, Wisborough Green

The Sounds Of The Sea

As the seahorses splash against the shore
The big waves toss and turn.
The seaweed dances and swirls around
Like a whirlpool.
You can hear the sea go splash
When children throw in pebbles.
The sea is like a diamond ring
Broken into pieces.
The ocean moving from morning to evening
It gets quieter and quieter every minute
Until silence at twilight.

Lucy McLoughlin (7)
Wisborough Green Primary School, Wisborough Green

The Warrior

I woke up to see a tree
Its many-fingered arms swaying
I felt the sun's warm smile
The hot sand's grasp pulling me in
I heard a sound nearby
I spun round to see
A river running behind me
I washed my face
Grabbed my spear
I was off to war.

Paul Slade (11)
Wisborough Green Primary School, Wisborough Green

The Night Monster - Haiku

Hiding by the door
Green and slimy giant feet
Oh! It's only Mum.

Tammy Harris (9)
Wisborough Green Primary School, Wisborough Green

On The Beach

Seashells tossing and turning,
Watching fish dancing and splashing.
The sound of waves roaring,
Watching the tide breaking.
Watching seagulls landing on the sea,
The smell of saltwater as I step in the sea,
Little pebbles floating on the water's edge,
Sand in-between my toes,
The crash of the waves hitting rocks.

Lucy Ansell (7)
Wisborough Green Primary School, Wisborough Green

Shiny Shells

When you hold shells against your ear
They sound like the tide or the sea.
When shells are wet they look like shiny stars!
When the shells are wet they smell like the sea.
The shells look beautiful.
Shells are as shiny as vases.
Shells look like sparkling gems when they are in the water.
The shells look like sapphires in water.
I find shells on the beach.

Lise Easton (8)
Wisborough Green Primary School, Wisborough Green

Waves Crawling Around My Feet

Waves crawling around my feet, feels prickly.
As I am swimming I take my first breath.
I taste saltwater.
People dancing like swirling waves.
The water about to touch my toes.
Dolphins jumping into the air.
Me on my own, collecting hermit crabs.

Mark Slade (8)
Wisborough Green Primary School, Wisborough Green

On The Beach

People playing in the sea,
Waves going through their legs,
The waves splashing on the children,
Little girls and boys playing in the sea,
They're on the beach with their mum and dad,
They're sunbathing,
Playing all sorts of games,
Like catching a ball, playing 'It',
Or catching people on the beach,
People going in the sea,
Because they want to have some fun.

Jade Osmaston (8)
Wisborough Green Primary School, Wisborough Green

On The Beach

As I was walking up the beach
I spotted my footprints on the ground.
Then I saw a crab
I picked up the crab
And took it to the sea
And dropped it in the water.
I walked on home.

Oscar Voaden (8)
Wisborough Green Primary School, Wisborough Green

The Sea

People dancing like swirling waves
Dolphins jumping in the air
People scuba-diving and touching fish
Waves swirling and splashing
Waves swirling like people
The sunset makes the sea beautiful.

Finn Spackman (8)
Wisborough Green Primary School, Wisborough Green

On The Beach

As I walk down the beach seagulls squawk
The water splashes like mad
The waves are like a giant bucket
The sun is like a shiny light
The sea is white horses
The sandcastles are like real homes
The water is like see-through jelly
The dolphins spin like twisted candyfloss
The waves are giant slides
The seaweed slimy goo
The salt is food spice
Today I will never forget the day, never.

Maxim Dillon (7)
Wisborough Green Primary School, Wisborough Green

On The Beach

I can see the waves roaring,
Swirling, tossing and turning,
Feel the seaweed wrap around your legs,
Hear the seagulls squawking their heads off,
Feel the crabs pinch you.

Watch sea horses curl their tails
Around the seaweed,
See the children splashing in the water,
Watch the white horses in the sea.

George Steere (8)
Wisborough Green Primary School, Wisborough Green

Anger

Fire engulfed my gut,
Anger, hatred burning fury,
The lowest of the low
Below the scum
Beneath the sewer
Lower than rats
The opposite of Zenith
Their rotted will
My soul eaten
My world destroyed
My brain swallowed by the hatred that is . . .
This evil world.

Ben Dadswell (11)
Wisborough Green Primary School, Wisborough Green

On The Beach

As I go past the sandcastles melt
As I got in the sea it swishes round me
In the rock pools fish swim
As I look for shells I find some seaweed
As I go by I see a broken anchor
In the water are primrose waves
As I walk out of the sea crabs click
My footprints have faded
When I look at the sky seagulls cry.

Violet Nicholls (7)
Wisborough Green Primary School, Wisborough Green

The Sea

As I am playing with Amelia
I hear the splish, splash of the sea.
My toes have sand on,
It came from the sea.
I look and see seagulls above me
It is a beautiful sight.
The sea waves are like unicorns dancing gracefully,
The waves are splashing
Like baby Amelia playing in water.
Water running round my toes
Today I'll never forget the sea.

Ami Gilfoyle (7)
Wisborough Green Primary School, Wisborough Green

On The Beach

Smelling saltwater like salt on chips,
Crashing waves along the beach,
Breezy wind being pushed away,
Sea horses over the sand,
Seagulls talking like mad,
Dribbly babies on the sand,
Seaweed pink and green,
Sand like sprinkled sugar,
Sea tossing and turning
Like dancers swirling,
Waves splashing and roaring,
Sea horses dazzling in the light,
Banging waves along the sand.

Richard Mason (8)
Wisborough Green Primary School, Wisborough Green

On The Beach

I saw the tide
Getting deeper
And deeper.
In the sea
I saw a tiny shell
Floating on the wave.
I picked it up
Out of the sea.
I saw the sea
Dancing like waves.
On the beach
I saw some seaweed
Tickly on my feet
It tickled my feet a lot.

Charlotte Gay (7)
Wisborough Green Primary School, Wisborough Green

On The Beach

As I am sitting on the beach
The waves get me wet.
I feel the sand,
I can smell ice creams and the sea.
I can hear the sea and the wind,
I can feel the sun.
I can see and hear seagulls,
I can see a crab.
The sea horses spilling over
When they hit the shore.

Jason Grove (7)
Wisborough Green Primary School, Wisborough Green

Listen To The Seashore

Feel the slushy sand in-between your toes
The waves like roaring white sea horses
Tossing and dancing in the rough sea
Listen to the tide tickling up your legs
Hear the shells and stones trickling down like sugar.

See the starfish so still and silent
Just sitting there,
Watching the seagulls pass by
Look at the sunset with mermaids and dolphins
Flying over the calm and soft sea.

Smell the soggy seaweed squished in-between
The spine of a red and yellow kite,
Feel the tide breaking in the middle of the Mediterranean sea.

Look at the children splashing in the glittering water
As shiny and as beautiful as a big diamond,
Smell the salt twirling in the ocean,
Each individual shell sitting on the sand
Like tiny stars in the black night.

Emily Usher (8)
Wisborough Green Primary School, Wisborough Green

Anger

Fury in my heart
Lungs on fire
Destroyed all over
Isolated
Layers of fury
Insignificant
Soul gone.

Tom Appleton (11)
Wisborough Green Primary School, Wisborough Green